Upgrade Now

Upgrade Now:
9 Advanced Leadership Skills

Giselle Kovary &
Adwoa K. Buahene
n-gen People Performance Inc.

ISBN – 978-1-77084-198-7

Printed in Canada
♻
on recycled paper

FIRST CHOICE BOOKS
DEMAND PUBLISHING & BINDING

www.firstchoicebooks.ca
Victoria, BC

10 9 8 7 6

Contents

Acknowledgements

We would like to thank the following clients for contributing to this book. Our discussions with you were very valuable in helping us to shape and confirm the direction of the content.

Arbor Memorial Services
Codi Shewan, Manager, Training & Development, Funeral Service
Jerry Roberts, Vice-President, Funeral Service

Best Buy Canada
Shannon Kidd, Senior Manager, Corporate Communications & Community Relations

Chevron
Sam Chow, Organizational Capability Team Lead

Cisco Canada
Ayelet Baron, Vice-President, Strategy and Transformation

Enerplus
Brien Perry, Vice-President, Human Resources

Freddie Mac
John Stickeler, Director - Office of Diversity & Inclusion

Government of Ontario
Conrad Brown, Director, Telecommunications Services Branch, MGS

Murphy Oil Company
Darrell Demick, Chief Reservoir Engineer

Scotiabank Group
Brian H. Toda, Senior Vice President, Global Talent Management

Acknowledgements

Shoppers Drug Mart
Darren Ratz, Vice President Human Resources

Starwood Hotels and Resorts Canada
Kim Gilliard, Regional Director Human Resources

TharpeRobbins
Susan Tolle, Senior Vice-President – Talent
Anthony Luciano, Senior Vice-President & Chief Marketing Officer

The Clorox Company of Canada
Lori Galati Aguiar, Director, Human Resources

Wal-Mart Canada
Curtis Mengler, Senior Manager, Engagement Strategy

Xerox Canada
Martine Normand, Vice-President Human Resources

No book is a singular effort; *Upgrade Now* could not have happened without the support of the n-gen team. Tracy Yan, your project management skills were tremendous in keeping us on track and ensuring a great design. Jocelyn Nsherenguzi, thank you for interviewing our clients to gather relevant examples and always providing meaningful suggestions. Jessica Francis, your hard work and enthusiasm as a research assistant was invaluable. Renee Wilson, your editing skills created a polished, finished product for our readers to enjoy. Thank you.

Why Upgrade Now?

In our fast-paced world, we are continuously upgrading the technology we use, where we live and work, and our professional skill sets. Today, leaders must adapt to a rapidly changing work environment. The status quo is not acceptable. To be successful, you need to upgrade your knowledge and expertise. This book is designed to provide you with the tools needed to attain an advanced understanding of how to lead your employees, which, in turn, will improve your ability to deliver business results.

> *It has been a long time since unbridled growth, readily accessible resources and a seemingly unlimited supply of easily satisfied customers were typical...(where) inexperienced, sloppy and even ineffective management could be hidden...managerial mistakes were overshadowed by constant increases in revenue and sales. The modern environment of organizations, however, is no longer benevolent. Razor sharp managerial leadership is required now just to stay even. Under conditions of lean resources, escalating competition, and hyper-turbulent change, management mistakes and inadequacies are often both visible and consequential. Never before has there been a period of time when effective managerial leadership is more crucial for organizational success."* [1]

To 'upgrade' means to build upon what already exists in order to enhance, improve and refine. It's not about discounting the old. Rather, it's about re-evaluating what works and what doesn't, and improving upon it. This process is on-going. You must be prepared to consistently upgrade your skills throughout your career. *Upgrade Now* supports this goal. The content is structured so that you can quickly reference any of the nine advanced leadership skills to deepen your knowledge. We have leveraged our expertise to bring you a practical, application-based book that layers on a generational perspective to each skill. Without a concrete understanding of how to adapt your leadership practices to meet the differing needs of a multigenerational workforce, you won't have fully upgraded. n-gen has worked with over 50,000 senior leaders, managers and employees since 2003. Our research, focusing on what employees want, and the challenges leaders face, has shaped this book. The generational perspective to each of the nine advanced leadership skills gives you the ability to upgrade what you do and how you do it.

The Four Generations

In our first book, *Loyalty Unplugged: How to Get, Keep & Grow All Four Generations,* we provided leaders and HR departments with strategies and tools to engage a multigenerational workforce. We addressed two key concepts – generational differences and engagement. We presented a model of organizational engagement that serves as the basis of our work.

The four generations are:

Traditionalist	1922 - 1945
Baby Boomer	1946 - 1964
Generation X	1965 - 1980
Generation Y	1981 - 2000

   While Traditionalists represent a very small percentage of our clients' workforces (approximately 1 - 3%), this generation remains an important cohort to consider. Given that their values and expectations are still deeply rooted in many organizational cultures, you need to consider their perspective when leading. In addition, many leaders remain traditionalist in their leadership style, and therefore must be self-aware of their approach before they can begin the process of change.

Engagement

Since employee engagement has a direct impact on financial results, all leaders should be interested in how they can increase the engagement levels of their teams. The negative impact of disengaged employees often outweighs the positive contributions made by high performers. From lost productivity, to the wearing down of other team members' motivation, the financial and non-financial costs are significant.

   n-gen's expertise is in layering on a generational perspective to increase engagement and performance. To effectively engage and motivate employees, generational similarities and differences need to be taken into account. n-gen defines engagement as *a productive relationship between an organization and its employees.*

To create an engaging relationship with employees, your organization, and you, as a leader representing your organization, must demonstrate the characteristics of organizational engagement. These characteristics are:

- **Transparency:** an organization and its leaders are open, honest and forthcoming with information. The motives and intentions are obvious. Information is shared freely with all levels and roles. The organization and its leaders highlight how responsibilities and/or accountabilities impact the big picture.

- **Responsiveness:** an organization and its leaders actively listen to employees, solicit their feedback, and are committed to taking action in a timely manner. The organization communicates what it can and cannot do to meet employee expectations, and proactively manages expectations.

- **Partnering:** an organization and its leaders recognize that employees are equal partners and investors in the business. Leaders seek a win-win relationship with all employee groups, and view themselves as part of the team, not outside of it, by acting collaboratively.

This book provides you with practical tools and techniques for how to become a more transparent, responsive and partnering leader. From creating a more engaging work environment, to collaboratively building an employee's career, to taking a partnering approach during the change management process, you will be able to identify the specific actions you can take to engage your multigenerational workforce. Each chapter is structured to provide you with the information required to *learn* an advanced skill, tips for how to *apply* it, the generational perspective to *upgrade* your leadership approach, and a tool for how to *execute*. This focus on learning, applying, upgrading and executing ensures that the content of the book is targeted, specific and practical in nature. Throughout, we highlight how our clients are upgrading their practices, by providing real-world examples from a range of industries. The last chapter of this book explores the 5th generation, the "Global Generation", who will begin to enter the workforce in four years, bringing with them a whole new set of expectations, desires and needs. This requires that leaders continue to be adaptable, by learning and broadening their skills to effectively lead the future workforce.

1

CREATING AN ENGAGING WORK ENVIRONMENT

Creating an Engaging Work Environment

LEARN

The biggest positive influence leaders can have in engaging their people is to make changes that improve their work environment. The work environment is comprised of all the experiences employees have, from their interaction with leaders and their colleagues, to the type of work they do, to the way in which they work, to the physical work space they occupy. Your work environment is the 'vibe' that is created in your offices and between all employees. It defines your organizational culture and represents your unique organizational DNA.

Creating a strong work environment requires a multi-faceted approach that involves senior leadership, managers and team members. For nearly a decade, through our vast range of client work, we have gathered reams of data regarding what employees want in their work environment. The key factors are:

- **Collaborative leadership:** Managers who possess genuine people skills, are action-oriented, and non-authoritarian

- **Empowerment:** The ability to make decisions, to have meaningful work, and to be creative

- **Teambuilding:** Company-sponsored events, networking with senior leaders, fun team activities

- **Flexibility:** Adaptable work arrangements, supportive work-life balance

Ultimately, the goal of an effective work environment is to increase employee engagement, because highly-engaged employees deliver better business results, while disengaged employees erode the bottom line and the customer experience. As an organization, it is imperative to solicit employee feedback on how well you are engaging employees. As a leader, you must be open to receiving feedback and creating an environment where employees feel safe to voice their challenges, concerns and suggestions for improvement.

> *Either you will manage your culture, or it will manage you. Simply stated, organizational culture is the way people think and act. Every organization has a culture, which either works for you or against you, it can make the difference between success and failure...optimizing your culture should command your attention every bit as much as your efforts to achieve performance improvements in manufacturing, research & development, sales and every other organizational discipline.[1]*

Types of Work Cultures

All work environments manifest an organization's culture or DNA. For our client Freddie Mac, it is defined as "the prevailing attitudes and sentiments of the employees that generate within the corporate culture." In Freddie Mac's work environment, employees take a tremendous amount of pride in their company's mission to help stabilize the nation's residential mortgage markets and expand opportunities for homeownership and affordable rental housing.

While an organization's work environment is usually driven by the most senior leaders, with a trickle-down effect to the rest of the employees, front line leaders can also influence their own distinct sub-culture or climate. "Effective leaders will understand the DNA of their organizational culture...what's driving people...what's going to keep them and what's going to motivate them. Employees are more apt to follow a leader that understands the important elements to keep their workforce engaged" (Freddie Mac). It is at the team level that front line leaders can have a tremendous impact on employee engagement levels. You may also be able to leverage a strong team culture to influence the broader organizational work environment.

The four most common types of work cultures are:

Hierarchal Culture

- Rational analysis and decision making
- Policies and procedures
- Accuracy and precision in work details
- Consistent processes to ensure quality, service and cost management
- Measurement systems with regular reporting

Market Driven Culture

- Competitiveness and success over competition
- Strong customer relationships
- Speed of responsiveness
- Intensity for world-class performance
- Results focused to drive high performance

Clan Culture

- Teamwork
- Strong relationships based on trust and openness
- People development through coaching, feedback, learning, and development
- Collaboration with colleagues and the community at large
- Caring for others in a compassionate and empathic way

Adaptable / Flexible Culture

- Innovation
- Creativity in new ideas and problem solving
- Entrepreneurial spirit
- Future-focused vision
- Change and continuous improvements
- Flexibility and agility to changing priorities and business needs[2]

While our clients' work cultures run the gamut from hierarchical to flexible and adaptable, we strongly recommend that leaders work within their teams to create a culture that is as open as possible.

At a macro level, an adaptable/flexible work culture ensures that:

- Employees clearly understand the direction of the business and how they contribute
- Organizational efficiencies are improved
- Leaders/managers take an active role in engaging their teams
- Employees understand where and how they can grow in the organization
- There is investment in learning and development experiences
- Swift action is taken to close the gap between the current state and desired future state

At a micro level, leaders can build an adaptable/flexible work culture by:

- Focusing on results
- Demonstrating emotional intelligence
- Empowering employees
- Rewarding and reinforcing the right behaviours
- Promoting flexibility
- Establishing cross-functional teams
- Integrating fun into the work environment
- Building trust

Excellent communication skills will underpin all of your actions. Communication must be open, transparent, and frequent enough to motivate, inform and inspire employees. Regardless of where your team is located – onsite or virtual – your role is to build a work environment that increases engagement and productivity.

APPLY

To build an engaging work environment, focus on the following seven factors:

1. Flexibility

If you can only focus on one area of improvement, building greater flexibility into your work environment is the best place to start. Organizations, big and small, private and public sector are focused on how to increase workplace flexibility because the cost savings of doing so (through increased retention and higher productivity) are significant. Employees who have even a small degree of flexibility in when and where work gets done have significantly greater job satisfaction, stronger commitment to their employer, higher levels of engagement, and lower levels of stress.[3]

Workplace flexibility is now viewed as a core business strategy, and not simply a 'nice to have'. U.S. President Barack Obama is quoted as saying "workplace flexibility isn't just a women's issue. It's an issue that affects the well-being of our families and the success of our businesses...it affects the strength of our economy – whether we'll create the workplaces and jobs of the future that we need to compete in today's global economy."[4]

To create a more flexible work environment, implement one or more of the following options:

Flex-time

- Employees select their start and end times within a range of core hours

Compressed work week

- Employees work their allotted hours over fewer days

Reduced time

- Employees can work part-time (which includes job sharing) or part-year, which may be full-time during school months and part-time when children are off from school

Flex-leaves

- Employees have access to time off to address personal or family issues

Flex-careers

- Employees have multiple points of entry, exit and re-entry over the course of their career

Flex-place

- Employees can work in places and times other than the standard work environment[5]

In working with Murphy Oil, we have seen firsthand how flexibility can be leveraged. Employees are able to work a 9/80 work schedule – 80 hours in 9 days within a 2 week period. This provides employees with the opportunity to control their work schedules so that they can balance other personal priorities, while meeting all deliverables.

Flexibility, however, is not just about where and when people come to work, it can also occur when employees are able to:

- Select their desired work assignments

- Schedule their own lunch/breaks

- Determine how a task gets done

- Choose involvement in special projects or committees

- Change a process to achieve a result or satisfy a customer/stakeholder need

Rather than it being seen as an employee perk, flexibility can be regarded as improving how work gets done. At Freddie Mac, leaders encourage employees to utilize flexible work arrangements. To enable this, managers are provided with a toolkit designed to assist them in developing solutions to overcome any potential obstacles associated with these types of work arrangements.

2. Empowerment

Empowerment is more than just giving employees 'permission' to make decisions. It is about creating a work environment where employees accept accountability and own decisions from beginning to end. Empowerment creates transparency and openness which enhances teamwork, trust and communication. Obstacles to empowerment are: work overload; lack of control; insufficient rewards relative to output; lack of team spirit; absence of fairness; and conflicting values between employees and the organization.[6]

You can empower employees by:

- Defining desired results

- Providing direction, support or coaching as required

- Rewarding positive behaviours

- Involving employees in the decision making process

- Building a sense of community through bi-weekly team events

- Delegating new tasks

- Soliciting feedback from employees on their preferred management style

At Best Buy Canada they empower their employees by giving them the 'space' to innovate through a strengths-based approach where employees are encouraged and supported to maximize their natural talents in their everyday work.

3. Recognition

Your ability to execute on your reward and recognition strategy will have an impact on how engaging your work environment is. Employees will not go above and beyond in their roles, if they feel that you don't appreciate their efforts and that you don't recognize their hard work. If you want outstanding results, you need to have an environment where you give as much as you take. Provide informal and formal recognition on an on-going basis. By building a strong relationship with your employees, you learn what is important to them, and therefore, can tailor your rewards to what is most valued to them. Non-monetary rewards, such as time off and support for community events that are important to employees, are great ways to formally recognize and appreciate contributions to the team. Thank you messages, flowers, and food are all easy, informal ways of recognizing individual or team performance. Focus your recognition efforts on reinforcing desired behaviours and results. This will motivate employees to concentrate on the right things and direct future behaviour.

4. Emotional Intelligence

The ability to inspire others, build loyalty and trust, and create a positive, supporting work environment is dependent on your ability to demonstrate emotional intelligence (EI), which is defined as "the ability to monitor one's own and others' feelings and emotions, to discriminate among them and to use this information to guide one's thinking and actions."[7]

You can demonstrate EI by:

- **Accurately perceiving emotions** – understand nonverbal signals such as body language

- **Reasoning with emotions** – using your emotions to promote thinking and cognitive activity by prioritizing what to focus on or react to

- **Understanding emotions** – being clear about the meaning of emotions. If an employee expresses an emotion (e.g. anger), you must be able to interpret the cause of the anger and what it might mean

- **Managing emotions** – regulating your own emotions and responding appropriately, as well as responding to the emotions of employees in an empathic way

5. Trust

All relationships are dependent on trust, be it personal or professional. Trust is a fundamental requirement for a high performing work environment and employee engagement. A trusting relationship also enhances innovation, creativity and collaboration. If employees trust you as a leader, they will be more likely to invest rationally and emotionally in their work, the team, and the organization.

Earning employees' trust is something that takes time and effort and it must come from a genuine interest and desire to connect with others.

You can build trust by:

- Following through on promises

- Being consistent with your word

- Treating all employees with fairness

- Living your corporate values day-to-day

- Being honest in all communications

- Leading by example

- Being a part of the team, not outside of it

- Asking employees what behaviours you demonstrate that build or erode trust and committing to improvement

6. Cross-Functional Collaboration

The opportunity to collaborate with colleagues in the same field or more broadly across the organization is critical to building an engaging work environment. Employees feel a sense of connection when they can share ideas with others, participate in group problem solving, and contribute to something bigger than themselves. In interviewing Best Buy Canada, we learned that its culture of collaboration is heavily based on cross-functional teams. These teams foster participation and open dialogue from all team members regardless of title or level.

Establishing cross-functional teams that work together to solve strategic business challenges is an excellent way to cultivate broader collaboration, especially if the team represents all departments and geographies in the organization. It's a win-win, in that employees have an opportunity to expand their network and work closely with new colleagues, and you reap the benefits of more brain power working together to solve your challenges. It also fosters an environment where employees work towards a common goal. Similar to empowering individual employees, you also need to empower cross-functional teams by setting goals for shared accountability and providing support through time, tools, resources and commitment.

> *"Cross-functional teams provide an exciting opportunity for the creation of a learning community. As teams bring together scientists from different disciplines, crafts people with different skills, employees from different functions, technical people with different specialties, and professionals from different countries, the learning possibilities are almost limitless. A community of self-directed learning and teachers, with everyone playing both roles, is established."* [8]

7. Fun at work

Some of the most profitable businesses, such as Google and Zappos, attribute their success to creating a fun work environment. By combining a focus on results, flexibility, and fun, leaders within these organizations ensure that cross-functional collaboration, creativity and team bonding flourish. In this type of work environment, fun is integrated into the work day. In fact, in many ways, the work itself is fun. This results in employees who work more enthusiastically and enjoy the process of work. At Best Buy Canada, their work environment is fun and engaging due to a wide range of services including a full service onsite gym that is open 24/7 that offers group fitness classes and individual personal training sessions. Also, a subsidized dining area is available where colleagues can meet informally and enjoy a range of healthy food options.

Regardless of your industry or department, there is always an opportunity to inject some fun into work. Murphy Oil has transformed their culture from a 'black and white organization to one that embraces fun, laughter and humour in the workplace.' By letting loose and having fun with colleagues, productivity and enthusiasm will be renewed. You'll also increase retention and profitability, while you reduce stress, anxiety, and boredom.[9] In addition, creativity can flourish, since time away from day-to-day tasks can spark a new perspective to an old problem. Each week at Google, they make it possible for employees to spend 30% of their time to work on fun, creative tasks that personally interest them. Not only does this make work more fun and interesting, it also translates into new, innovate projects that have yielded financial success.[10]

Despite the evidence to support the positive effects of a fun work environment, many leaders still believe that fun is something that should happen after work hours and that it's a distraction from productivity. You may need to overcome resistance from other leaders who don't support your desire to inject fun into the work-place.

To spark fun into your work environment, and encourage other leaders to follow your lead, you should:

- Celebrate hard work on the spot and in the moment by giving colleagues a standing ovation

- Be spontaneous by interrupting work with a fun activity

- Encourage humour and laughter – be light-hearted

- Don't control fun or make rules – expand what it means to have fun at work

- Ask employees what is fun to them and then let them do it

- Empower employees to plan and implement fun events, such as a comedian of the month that shares his/her all-time most humorous stories

UPGRADE

For our clients, there is an intense focus on understanding what needs to be done to create a more engaging work environment, particularly for younger employees since the need to recruit, retain and engage these cohorts is high. Creating an engaging work environment for Gen Xers and Gen Ys involves a combination of factors, including: management practices; work options; rewards; and team activities. The most important factor to Gen Xers and Gen Ys in creating a desirable work environment is having an open and collaborative culture. Gen Xers respond best to a market-driven culture, since this cohort focuses on results and outcomes. Gen Ys find an adaptable work culture most attuned to their needs, since it provides the greatest opportunity for creativity and innovation.

Greater flexibility has also been cited by many of our corporate managers as a way to meet employees' desires for a work-life balance. Flex hours, working from home, and flexible work spaces were all highlighted as ways leaders can engage Gen Xers and Gen Ys. Managers must also empower their teams to make decisions by delegating meaningful work to them and trusting their abilities. Micro-management immediately disengages Gen Xers, who like to work independently. Gen Ys also become disengaged by this management style, because it doesn't allow them to be creative and innovative in their roles. Gen Ys desire lots of open communication, with 60% citing they want to hear from their manager at least once a day.[11]

The goal of Generation Y is to find work and create a life that has meaning. Thus, it is very important that the work they do be connected to the big picture. Younger employees must understand the meaningfulness of the work they do in the organization, with customers and with the community at large. Gen Xers seek meaning in their work based on whether or not they are fully utilizing their capabilities and skills. Meaningful work to Gen Xers are projects that contribute to tangible results and which are challenging to them.

It is also important to understand the current and evolving needs of experienced employees and how to meet them. If your organization is traditionalist in nature and the work environment is hierarchical, this may be acceptable for many of your Traditionalist employees (or employees who possess a Traditionalist mind-set), since this cohort is accustomed to working in top-down, authoritative environments. Nevertheless, consider how you can incorporate greater flexibility into their work day. Many of our clients find that experienced employees are equally eager for part-time, flexible schedules and seasonal work. Your Baby Boomers respond best to an environment that is collaborative in nature and provides flex-leaves to allow them to tend to the needs of aging parents or child-care issues. They are the most engaged when working in a clan work culture where collaboration, caring and strong relationships are paramount. At Freddie Mac, one of their seven employee network groups focuses on the needs of those in the 'sandwich' generation – employees who face the challenges associated with caring for young children and/or aging family members. They have created tools and resources for employees such as a caregiver's guide, offer ongoing workshops and seminars focused on relevant care giving and work life balance topics, and provide support groups to share and learn from one another.

It is important to recognize that as you try to move your culture to a more adaptable one, some of your experienced workers may struggle with the changes. They may either prefer the current culture or they may feel that their desires for a more formal and structured work culture are no longer being respected. They may feel that the 'young' are changing things too quickly. Make allowances for this transition period and respect their desire to continue to work in their preferred style. By being transparent and employing change management techniques to help them transition to a more dynamic environment, you will be able to engage them more quickly.

Since your team is likely comprised of two or three generations, consider how you can incorporate elements of the different types of work cultures to create a unique environment that motivates, engages and propels your team forward. Leverage the different techniques for empowerment to drive greater business results. Focus on building trust with all generations through open and honest dialogue, frequent touch points, and soliciting employee opinions. These core skills will set you up for success and will create the best environment for all employees to excel.

EXECUTE

The following tool will assist you in identifying your current work-place culture and what actions you can take to make it more engaging for all employee groups. You can also slightly modify this tool and use it as an informal survey to conduct with your team.

Questions	Responses

Your leadership style is most typical of:

- Hierarchal Culture

- Market Driven Culture

- Clan Culture

- Adaptable / Flexible Culture

Your perceptions of work are most aligned to:

"work hard" – *employees shouldn't have a good time at work, that's why it's called work!*

"be seen" – *employees should always appear to be busy and be visible with lots of face time and long hours in the office.*

"don't push back" – *employees shouldn't rock the boat or challenge the status quo.*

"us versus them" – *separate business units or teams should compete against each other.*

"old school" – *employees are considered to be family, leaders should act as the parents.*

Questions	Responses
What is working well in your current work environment?	
What do you want to change about your work environment?	
What do you want to continue to do?	
Which of the seven success factors are your strongest at? 1. Flexibility 2. Empowerment 3. Recognition 4. Emotional intelligence 5. Trust 6. Cross-functional collaboration 7. Fun at work	
What is one success factor you can improve on? What actions will you take to improve?	
How can you ensure your work environment engages the different generations on your team?	

2 FACILITATING EMPLOYEES' CAREER DEVELOPMENT

Facilitating Employees' Career Development

LEARN

In the workplace, the word 'career' is used all the time by leaders. They often make normative comments about how they see colleagues, employees and managers approach their careers, as in 'that move was a career killer', or 'didn't she think about how it will impact her career'? What is being presupposed is that everyone is defining the concept of 'career' the same way, and that there is only one way to achieve a successful career. While that may have been true 15-20 years ago, it's no longer the case that there is a uniform definition of the concept of a career. Organizations no longer guarantee life-time job security through traditional career-paths, having placed the responsibility on employees to manage their own careers. In response to these changes, employees have developed alternate ways to build a successful career that suits their motivations and desires. Technology, outsourcing, globalization, contract work and generational expectations have morphed jobs and careers into varied forms. In today's dynamic work world, leaders must demonstrate skills to help employees build their desired career-paths. In order to be successful, you need to realise that you are not managing employees' careers, but rather, you are facilitating them along their desired paths.

The objective of any career development conversation or career management process is to keep employees longer. That means either longer tenure within the team, or longer tenure within the organization. Leaders need to recognize that gone are the days when they can rely on employees remaining in the organization for their entire career, or that employees will simply follow the career-path determined by the organization. While career-paths are still important for organizations to develop from a strategic standpoint, those career-paths act only as a framework/guideline for leaders. More importantly, leaders need to *understand* their employees' definition of a career, *assist* employees in realising that definition, and *act* to remove barriers so that employees can achieve their career goals. As our client, Enerplus, stated: "sometimes HR tries to make it too scientific, with career ladders, competency matching programs, etc. which are all good tools, but not all that helpful if the leader isn't really sitting down, looking the employee in the eye, and asking them what they want to do next, where they want to be in five years and what they can do to help them get there."

Career Development Paths

Historically, the traditional career-path contained small, incremental, upward moves over ones' life[1] or "a series of upward moves, with steadily increasing income, power, status, and security."[2] As the nature of business has changed, employees have increasingly been charged with managing their own careers. Over time, the ways in which employees define ideal career-paths have morphed from a traditional approach, to a more transitory one. The four types of career-paths are:

The Linear Career-Path

- A linear, hierarchy-based, career-path is one in which employees work hard, and over time rise up a predictable path to the next level on a vertical corporate ladder, until they can no longer climb to another level. Generally, this type of path includes moving into leadership positions, whether or not the employee wants to become a people leader. Today, this is not the only desired or available option for many employees. In fact, the odds of employees pursuing this path are becoming less and less likely.

The Expert Career-Path

- This career-path rewards the development of skills in a specific field of expertise without making it necessary to move upward into management levels. Positions commonly don't have people leadership responsibilities, but include hierarchical designations such as trainee, associate, junior, senior, etc. particularly in organizations that employ knowledge-based employees. This path has changed core, stable workforces into highly skilled, mobile and adaptable workforces.

The Spiral Career-Path

- The spiral career-path allows employees to make a series of lateral moves between different functional areas within the same organization. It allows human resource departments to focus on retaining talent by continuously providing employees with new and challenging tasks that broaden their experience while, at the same time, limiting swift hierarchical progression.

The Transitory Career-Path

- The hallmark of the modern-day employee is the transitory career-path, which usually allows employees to avoid depending on any one organization. Employees build and maintain a portfolio of competencies, allowing them to respond quickly to changes in the job market.

- Employees move in and out of organizations and roles in search of better jobs, building up an arsenal of skills in the process. Employees rarely rely on formal employer provided career planning. Instead, they manage their own careers. However, it is critical that leaders learn how to hold career development discussions with these employees to keep them longer, by helping them to build their portfolio within the organization.[3]

Employee Career Patterns

As it relates to what motivates employees in their careers, the research indicates that individual employees tend to place more emphasis on internal, psychological career drivers, rather than on organizational success. They seek greater autonomy over their own career development.[4] "In the context of the twenty-first century workplace, a career is viewed as the property of a person, rather than an occupation or an organization."[5] So it is employees who own their careers, who are responsible for the success or failure within it, not the organization or a regulatory body (e.g. engineering, law, healthcare etc). Experts describe employees' motivations for autonomy as a desire to become either *specialists*, *generalists* or *entrepreneurial*. These patterns align nicely to the four career paths described above.[6]

The *specialist pattern* involves careers that have a strict adherence to a particular occupational field, which requires specialized education, knowledge and skills. This means that career moves are relatively vertical and predictable. Employees who would be considered 'specialists' fit nicely into the expert career-path, because they are motivated by formal, predictable career moves that require very specialized knowledge and skills. However, specialists do not necessarily have a specific desire to manage others. They'd rather manage their own projects. This differentiates them from those who are interested in the traditional, linear career path.

In the **generalist pattern**, there are usually a number of back-and-forth horizontal career moves. This pattern is suitable for someone who is looking to build a larger foundation of expertise and networking opportunities with other professionals. Employees who have more generalist motivations fit nicely into the spiral career-path, because they are more interested in horizontal moves in order to broaden their skill sets and be able to network.

An **entrepreneurial pattern** is characterised by frequent career moves, a high degree of mobility, little adherence to formality, and deep expertise over a range of interests. Employees with entrepreneurial motivations fit best in a transitory career-path, because they are most interested in frequent career moves, possess high levels of mobility and have the ability to expand their expertise broadly.

In any of the four types of career-paths, or in the corresponding employee motivations, the responsibility for success becomes a shared responsibility between the employee, the organization, and the leader. First, organizations need to either build all three types of career paths, or at least be transparent as to which paths are available and possible. Next, employees need to be able to individually identify which path best aligns to their career motivations, and in which they would excel. Then, leaders need to assess career motivations with their employees, and be able to help facilitate success.

As a leader, you need to evaluate whether or not all four types of career paths (traditional, expert, spiral or transitory) are possible in your organization. Does your organization encourage, support and value each path equally, if chosen by an employee? Your role in helping employees develop their careers is not paternalistic, but rather facilitative, acting as a sounding board for ideas and assisting in the removal of barriers. "A facilitator creates conditions for others' success. A facilitator helps reduce dependence and increases employee independence as employees seek their career goals. Effective facilitation requires developing a relationship of trust between the facilitator and the participant."[7] It is your responsibility to build an open, honest relationship with your employees, so that they feel comfortable sharing their career aspirations. Accomplish this by talking about the various career/job changes you have made, or by acknowledging that it is rare that employees in today's work world stay with one organization forever. Also, collect and share success stories of how employees have been able to follow each (or some) of the career path options within your organization.

Leaders have to be careful not to become barriers themselves to their employees' success. In this resource-hungry age, leaders are sometimes reluctant to assist high-performing, high-potential employees from moving on, because they are more worried about meeting quarterly or yearly goals than they are about developing and encouraging career-paths for their employees.[8] With our client, Enerplus, leaders are charged with viewing employees as a company resource, rather than a departmental resource.

Career Development Conversations vs. Performance Management Conversations

It is important that we distinguish between career development conversations and performance management reviews. In performance management, leaders identify performance gaps and the competencies required to improve performance. In career development conversations, the focus is on what paths employees want their careers to take, and whether or not the organization and its leaders can (and want to) assist employees in traveling down that path. It makes sense that, if employees are high performing, you and your organization will do whatever you can to help that employee achieve his/her career goals, especially when they align with the operational needs and goals of the organization and team. However, if an employee's desired path does not align with organizational goals, it still might be prudent for you to help him/her develop competencies and skills that are operationally relevant, until that employee moves on.

Knowing that employees are seeking a different career direction than the organization offers, does not mean that employees cannot be a good match in the current state. At Enerplus, leaders are encouraged to have open career development conversations. "Even if you feel you can't provide what employees need (want) within our company, it's better to know what they need and where they want to go, and support them where you can, rather that employ the head in the sand, ostrich approach (of ignoring their desires)."

APPLY

Below are tips and techniques for conducting a successful career development conversation. You initially need to set the stage with employees by building a trusting relationship. Then, like any business meeting, you need to evaluate the possibilities and plan for the conversation. Lastly, you need to act as a facilitator in order to help employees build their careers.

- Create and send your career development questions to employees in advance of your conversation, so that they can reflect and evaluate how they would like their career to evolve. Ask them to come prepared to the meeting with answers to your questions. A career development conversation should be treated with the same seriousness as any other type of business or performance review meeting.

- Discuss specialist, generalist or entrepreneurial career patterns. You should collaboratively explore employees' career goals to determine their likely pattern. Be prepared to tell them the opportunities and barriers to following each pattern within your organization. Discuss how they can overcome the barriers (with your support) in order to assist them in continuing to develop their skills within and beyond their current role (if possible).

- Identify the skills the employees want to develop, and whether they are short, medium, or long-term developmental goals (make sure you are on the same page as to what 'short, medium, long-term' means as far as monthly/yearly timeframes). Make plans to help employees develop the identified skills through peer mentoring, coaching, training, job shadowing, reading, volunteering, etc. Be creative in how they can develop the desired skills. These plans are over and above any competencies or skills that are included in a development plan determined within the performance management process.

- Encourage employees to take on new tasks and projects that are outside of their comfort zone in order to help them develop the skills necessary for their desired career path. For example, if an employee is reluctant to speak in front of others, but would like to become more confident in order to move into a more senior position, then have her/him prepare a presentation on her/his latest assignment and present it to you first, and then colleagues, and then someone more senior, in order to practice and develop that new skill.

- Have career development conversations with all employees, not just high-performing/high-potential ones. Employees who are average/mid-range performers are still essential to your team and to the organization. It's important to consider that those not categorized as high-potential may actually be looking for a different type of career-path, but might not know how to build the necessary skills. You can increase engagement levels of moderately engaged employees by not necessarily focusing on a specific career move, but rather focusing on the skills, competencies, or simply 'things they want to learn'.

- Be a career connector. If you don't know how to help employees with their career goals, facilitate an introduction to HR, another department, or another colleague who might be able to assist or provide guidance. Collaborating with employees in achieving their career development goals builds trust, increases engagement and results in greater loyalty.

UPGRADE

It is vitally important for you, as a leader, to be able to have meaningful career development conversations. From a generational perspective, you must understand both the past experiences employees might have had, as well as the changing definition of a career. Traditionalists and many Baby Boomers might be reluctant to be open and honest about their career goals because: 1) They are used to having the organization direct their career, by telling them what their next move will be and when it will occur; 2) They are inclined to adjust their message to what they think leaders want to hear; and 3) They may be worried about career retribution, if their career desires and thinking do not align with yours.

Many leaders tie loyalty with career goals. If an employee doesn't want his/her career to remain with the same team, organization or even industry, the leader judges the employee as being disloyal. For Traditionalists and Baby Boomers, it is important that you gain their trust, so that they will feel comfortable enough to be honest with you about their career goals. Also, experienced employees benefit the most from receiving career development discussion questions in advance, because it allows them the opportunity to craft their responses. Make sure to highlight that there are no right or wrong answers to these questions, but rather that they are a starting point for the discussion.

Your Gen X employees, and particularly your Gen Ys, have little trepidation telling leaders their career desires. In fact, you might be surprised at the candour of the conversation. It is important, when having career conversations with Gen Xers, to not take personal offence to any comments. Given their goal of maintaining professional independence, Gen Xers are often very 'clinical' as it relates to developing skills, learning and growing, and getting results. The best approach is one of negotiation. Be honest about what you or the organization can or cannot offer, as it relates to career development opportunities. Challenge your Gen Xers to propose ways that they can develop their desired career skills within their current roles. For many Gen Xers, they look to move up the corporate ladder because they think that is the only way that they can develop the skills they desire. Gen Xers tend to be open to a spiral career-path, or to remaining within their current role for a short-period of time, as long as they are developing desired skills.

A greater percentage of Gen Ys are likely to pursue a transitory career-path. This cohort was once nicknamed 'serial retirees', because they come in and out of the workforce as it fits their needs. They, too, are candid about their desired career-paths, but may be less realistic as to the speed by which it can happen in your organization. It is important to paint a clear picture of which career paths are possible within your organization, and to help Gen Ys identify their career motivations. This cohort may confuse moving up the corporate ladder with the development of skills, so you should spend time discussing how they can develop desired competencies in their current role. Also explain how each competency has different levels of skill demonstration (from fundamental to advanced). Gen Ys respond most effectively, and have high levels of engagement, when you work in collaboration with them by soliciting their feedback, respecting their career desires, and working with them to develop action plans. Any paternalistic judgement of their choices, based on a traditionalist viewpoint, will disengage them.

EXECUTE

When conducting career development conversations, take into consideration the following factors:

- The employee's length of employment
- The employee's stage within their career (early, mid-, late career)
- The employee's generational expectations

The following questions will assist you in having open career development discussions. The objective is to learn as much as possible about your employees' career expectations and desired goals. You will then need to either manage their expectations honestly, or discuss how you can support them in achieving their career goals, given your organization's operational reality. Each question is carefully constructed to solicit different responses, meaning the actions required will differ depending on the answer.

Career Development Questions

1. What are your strengths? Would you like to coach or mentor others on your skill strengths?

2. What cross-functional skills are you looking to build?

3. What type of projects would you like to lead/be involved in?

4. What would be a stretch assignment for you?

5. What do you want to *learn* in the next six months/year?

6. What *non role-specific competencies* would you like to *learn* (e.g. presentation, leadership, business acumen, strategy etc.)

7. What would be a *win* for you in the next year or 2 years?

8. What do you want your career to look like 5 years from now?

9. Is there another department in which you like to *gain some experience*? If yes, which one? Why? How?

10. Is there a department or a role you'd like to *learn* more about? If yes, which one? Why does it interest you?

11. What types of projects do your friends / colleagues in the industry work on that you think are interesting?

12. What gives your role *meaning*?

3

GENERATING RESULTS THROUGH PERFORMANCE MANAGEMENT

Generating Results Through Performance Management

Leaders often struggle with performance management. Some struggle with the 'science' of it, in that they don't know how to implement their organization's processes. Others are clear on what they need to do, but find it difficult to execute the 'art' of performance management, in that they don't know how to effectively conduct performance conversations and follow-up to ensure improved performance. Performance management (PM) can be defined in a number of ways, but at its core, the process is designed to deliver business results through high-performing employees. A comprehensive definition is:

> *"...a systematic process of improving organizational performance by developing the performance of individuals and teams. It is a means of getting better results from the organization, team and individuals by understanding and managing performance within an agreed framework of planned goals, standards and competence requirements. Processes exist for establishing a shared understanding about what is to be achieved, and for managing and developing people in a way that increases the probability that it will be achieved...it is owned and driven by line management."* [1]

Fundamentally, all PM processes are designed to: establish measureable goals for employees; assess achievement and attainment of the goals; and improve performance through coaching, development, and rewards. While each of these outcomes has processes attached to them, the success in achieving the outcomes lies in the 'art' of performance management. The most effective approach is to be transparent and future-oriented. Transparency is required to ensure that employees are clear about the process and purpose, as well as what is expected of them. Being future-oriented means setting goals for what employees should achieve, and then working collaboratively to achieve those outcomes. At its best, PM means working in partnership with employees to improve future performance, which will involve meaningful feedback, collaborative problem solving, and motivation.

The PM process allows organizations to maintain and increase productivity. It also yields benefits to leaders, including:

Building bench strength

- High-performing employees can fill key positions, thus enhancing succession planning

Increasing engagement and motivation

- Employees who have the opportunity to develop and achieve career progression will be more highly engaged and motivated, thus improving retention

Accepting accountability

- Poor performing employees will have the opportunity to improve and take ownership for outcomes, rather than simply receiving disciplinary action

Identifying top talent

- Employees can express their career aspirations and future goals, thus improving future workforce planning

Adding value

- Having the right employees, in the right roles, at the right time, will add value to the organization and internal / external customers

As highlighted, PM is more about people than systems or processes. It's about effectively managing employees, working with them to achieve a desired outcome, and supporting them to become productive employees:

> *Effective performance management is both an art and science. The people we work with are pieces of a complex puzzle which challenge our ability to solve problems. Individual performance management techniques are part of our toolkit. When we use them well and together, we can create a positive workplace experience.*[2]

Consistency in the execution of the PM process can be an operational challenge. Our client, Wal-Mart, has found that they must balance the need for autonomy at the store level with executing a standardized approach, in order to recognize the same employee behaviours across the organization. They achieve this by providing comprehensive tools that can be used by all leaders, at all levels.

Often leaders don't manage employee performance in a systematic way because there is a:

- Lack of comfort with evaluating employee performance levels
- Misunderstanding of the leader's role and requirements in the PM process
- Frustration with the complexity of PM systems
- Lack of knowledge of how to effectively manage performance

Following a standardized process is helpful in setting expectations for leaders and employees, and for the achievement of those expectations. For individual accountability to take root, leaders must set clear performance expectations; provide feedback; measure performance; and, communicate the rewards for good performance and the consequences of poor performance.

APPLY

You can effectively drive high performance in your teams by:

- Planning - set goals and objectives
- Managing - monitor progress and provide regular feedback and coaching
- Assessing - conduct a formal review process
- Rewarding - pay for performance, merit increases

Planning

To ensure that employees are clear about how they contribute to organizational performance, it is imperative that you provide them with a clear picture of how their actions help or hinder the organization's results. Leaders must cascade each level of the organization's goals in order to align each employee's role.

The process of goal setting helps employees identify where they can add the greatest value. It creates a free flow of communication about your strategy, goals and objectives. "An important consequence of the goal flow-down process, and improving the line of sight (for employees), is that information is no longer power because information becomes a commodity in the company."[3] Employees who understand what they need to do (behaviours /actions/tasks) to make the organization more successful are armed with the information they need to make smart decisions. Performance goals must be clear and linked to solid metrics in order to fairly assess performance.

There are four types of goals:

1. **Job Goals**
   - Directly related to job description/responsibilities

2. **Project Goals**
   - Related to special projects above and beyond routine tasks

3. **Professional Development Goals**
   - Related to the learning and development that will take place

4. **Performance Improvement Goals**
   - Behaviours and actions that must be met when poor performance exists

For each employee that you manage, identify which type of goal should be achieved and work in partnership with him/her to set a measurable outcome. If performance goals can't be easily quantifiable, then you must focus on competencies and behaviours. Ideally, competency descriptors and observable behaviours should be created for all employee goals, which will form the basis of your performance evaluation. The competencies and observable behaviours' describe *how* the employee should achieve their performance goals. You should collaborate with employees to create these competencies and observable behaviours. This provides clarity around performance expectations and ensures you gain buy-in up front.

> *The goal of the planning stage is to clarify the job expectations and to set goals with employees collaboratively.*

Managing

Once employees understand what needs to be achieved and have clear goals that they will be measured against, your role is to manage their performance by monitoring their progress and coaching them to success. PM is an on-going process that takes place throughout the year, rather than just during the annual appraisal period. It is a continuous cycle of evaluation, feedback and coaching, where you provide employees with tools that help them to succeed and to overcome obstacles.

You should collect objective data on your employees' performance, but also encourage your employees to keep their own performance record. This activity reinforces mutual accountability within PM. If gaps exist, learning, development and coaching programs should act as the framework for you and your employees to create a performance improvement plan. Throughout the year, you should conduct informal and formal performance discussions with an aim to reinforce employees' accountabilities, clarify goals and review the tools required to succeed. Fostering an environment where communication is central to your team culture, rather than just during performance review discussions, is the most effective way to manage employee performance. Both leaders and employees should be in alignment, mutually agreeing on the desired results and performance rating. At the end of the year, there shouldn't be any surprises.

The cornerstone of PM is coaching. Our client, Arbor, has shifted their culture around PM from one that was based on yearly reviews to a bi-annual process. There are frequent one-on-one coaching sessions, and the use of 360 degree assessments. To build a high performing team, you must be an effective coach that creates a trusting environment where continuous feedback is given and received.

Focus your efforts on coaching, rather than managing by:

- Exploring an issue versus telling what the issue is

- Facilitating employee reflections instead of directing what to do

- Demonstrating partnering-based leadership instead of authority-based leadership

- Focusing on long-term improvements instead of immediate needs

- Exploring a variety of possible outcomes versus a specific outcome[4]

Peter Drucker noted that in the 20th century, great leaders gave great answers; in the 21st century, great leaders will ask great questions. In an organizational setting, as is the case in professional sports, leaders may not necessarily be as adept or knowledgeable of the areas requiring coaching, as the person who is being coached. Thus becoming an expert on "the answers" is now, and will continue to be, all but impossible. The effective coach is one who questions and listens. Insightful questions lead to reflection; they lead to self-discovery.[5]

> *The goal of the managing stage is to monitor progress towards established goals and to provide feedback and coaching to ensure successful completion of all goals.*

Assessing

If you have provided ongoing, effective feedback, then the quarterly (or annual) performance rating will not be a surprise to employees. Performance reviews tend to fail when they are too heavily focused on the past, rather than the future. While it is important to identify problematic behaviours from the past, the focus of a performance review discussion should be on how to overcome them.

In the assessment phase, you will conduct a formal performance review. Depending on your organization's performance management process, you may need to complete a number of activities. At Chevron, the focus is on performance-based leadership, which requires leaders to evaluate not only whether performance targets are met, but also the behaviours employees demonstrate to achieve their goals. To ensure objective data is collected, leaders engage customers, clients and teams for feedback on each employee to assess his/her performance.

At the end of a performance review discussion with an employee, you should have:

- Confirmed scope of role/responsibilities

- Provided your observations of his/her performance

- Identified suggestions for improvement

- Listened to employee comments on his/her self-assessment

- Solicited suggestions from the employee on how you can collaborate together to improve performance

- Identified barriers to success and how to overcome them

- Completed all forms/paperwork required

- Documented decisions, discussions, and recommendations for pay, promotion, or disciplinary action[6]

The assessment phase can sometimes be difficult for leaders, because it may involve providing negative or developmental feedback. One way to avoid having a difficult performance review discussion is to ensure that you have communicated sufficiently throughout the year and that performance issues are addressed just-in-time, when they occur. The use of effective questioning is also particularly important when dealing with poor performance. The use of open-ended questions is best to elicit insight from employees. For example, you can ask: "How has your performance improved in the last few months? What areas do you think you still need to work on?" By having employees self-evaluate, the focus is inward and they are more likely to be open to 360 degree feedback. Questions that encourage evaluation, reflection, and critical thinking promote a deeper dialogue and result in a future focused discussion. This is truly where the 'art' of PM distinguishes leaders who are able to engage employees. Being able to create an open environment, where the conversation is free-flowing, emotions are acknowledged, assessments are objectively discussed, and action plans are created, is the hallmark of a successful PM process.

> *The goal of the assessment stage is to rate performance levels and achievement towards established goals, and document future action plans for learning and competency development.*

Rewarding

To have a high-performing team that delivers business results, you must provide recognition and rewards that motivate your team. Rewarding employee performance means giving both monetary and non-monetary rewards. While you may choose to reward your team as a group, it is also important to provide recognition of high performance at an individual level in order to reinforce accountability.

Effective PM motivates high-performers to remain on track, since they feel that their efforts are being recognized. It persuades poor performers to improve, since there are negative outcomes if they don't adjust their behaviour. Pay for performance "sends a clear message from management that the contributions of employees are valued and appreciated."[7]

> *The goal of the rewarding stage is to reward desired behaviours and actions to encourage high-performance from all employees.*

UPGRADE

From a generational perspective, each cohort's willingness to embrace PM is based on its comfort level with receiving feedback. Since working with us, Arbor has embraced a generationally focused approach to their PM process by acknowledging the differing values and perspectives that the four generations have towards the process.

Most Traditionalists experienced a work environment where the only performance feedback given was either really good news — 'you're getting promoted!' — or really bad news — 'you're getting fired!' This generation has only recently been exposed to organizational cultures where on-going feedback and setting performance goals are the norm. It can sometimes be difficult for Traditionalists to adapt to the current approach, since they have been working for many years without any formal performance review process. An annual performance review discussion is aligned with the comfort level for this cohort. If they want more feedback, they'll ask for it. They expect management to be directive, so they may be less comfortable and require more support on how to approach a more collaborative PM process.

Since the widespread use of PM metrics has only occurred in the last decade or so, many Baby Boomers are receiving formal performance reviews late in their careers. In the past, their performance was often commented on by senior leaders in a more informal way. Rewards were often largely based on the subjective perceptions of leaders (who you knew), versus the objective measurements to business outcomes (what you did). This approach sometimes left strong performers who didn't play the political game with little acknowledgement or recognition for their contributions. On the flip side, poor performers who were well connected within the organization were allowed to remain, or were even promoted. The PM process was secretive. It didn't necessarily provide employees with a clear understanding of why their performance was above or below standard.

Baby Boomers tend to down-play their weaknesses and eagerly highlight their strengths; for fear that discussing areas of weakness may jeopardize their position within the organization. Historically, performance discussions with Baby Boomer employees focused on what they accomplished and achieved (their wins), followed by feedback on areas of development/improvement, followed by a positive summary on how they are contributing to organizational and departmental goals. This sandwich model of feedback – positive, negative, positive – ensured performance discussions were positive in tone. A formal PM process that is done annually or bi-annually matches the comfort level of this cohort. They appreciate being included in the decision making process, and are more open to your feedback if you engage them in the conversation by allowing them to provide feedback on their performance.

In contrast, Gen X employees expect to receive feedback on their performance more frequently, on a quarterly or monthly basis. They don't want to spend a lot of time focusing on what they do well. They already know that. They want to understand how they can improve. This cohort wants to hear constructive feedback on their performance. Leaders should provide specific examples of what they would like Gen Xers to improve on and a deadline for those improvements. They need to know how success will be measured, and what resources and support will be provided to them. Gen Xers desire this type of feedback, because they want to remain marketable. They know they need to continuously improve, learn and grow. Performance discussions should focus on desired results (achievement of goals) from both your perspective and theirs, and should be concretely linked to career goals and individual development plans.

Gen Ys are even more eager to receive feedback. They expect to know how they are performing on a monthly, weekly, and daily basis. Though this generation has a large appetite for feedback, they are often ill prepared to receive negative criticism. Growing up in a school system and home life with high expectations, this generation fears failure. Also, this cohort has always received positive, self-esteem building praise by parents, teachers and coaches on an on-going basis. They haven't been accustomed to receiving negative feedback, nor are they well prepared for how to respond to such feedback. Receiving less than 100% (exceptional) on a performance rating may cause an emotional response in some Gen Ys. Managers should be trained to conduct performance discussions with Gen Ys that highlight developmental opportunities, without plummeting motivation and engagement levels. Also, you should be prepared to discuss and justify your performance ratings, in particular if Gen Y employees score themselves higher in their self-assessments than you score them.

Be aware that Gen Ys openly share their PM ratings and discussions with their peers. Our clients have had pairs or groups of Gen Ys who have wanted to discuss their performance evaluations together with their leader. Be prepared and open to having these types of discussions with younger employees. Refusing to engage in a conversation about performance will lead to employee disengagement, and mistrust. From a human resources perspective, it is not advisable to discuss any one employee's performance with another employee or group, but you can use team meetings to reinforce desired competencies, and to brainstorm actions that the group can take to demonstrate desired behaviours.

EXECUTE

As a leader, you are ultimately accountable for how your team performs and for the contribution you collectively make to your organization's success. This tool is designed to help you prepare for and conduct effective performance discussions, and to ensure that the final year end performance rating isn't a surprise.[8]

Evaluation Checklist	Yes	No
1. Do you understand the employee's role, level of performance and challenges s/he faces?		
2. Have you reviewed the employee's performance plan to ensure that the performance goals are still relevant?		
3. Did you engage in routine discussions with the employee throughout the year about his/her achievements, challenges and areas of improvement?		
4. Have you documented examples of successful performance and opportunities for improvement?		
5. Have you assessed whether the areas of opportunities are based on a lack of knowledge, skill or attitude, to help prepare a performance improvement plan?		

Evaluation Checklist	Yes	No

6. Have you recognized or rewarded the employee throughout the year for high performance?

7. Have you solicited feedback from other stakeholders on the employee's performance?

8. Have you asked the employee for his/her self-assessment of the performance rating?

9. Have you identified how you will adapt your approach to the performance management process to align with the employee's generational expectations?

10. Have you identified potential areas of disagreement you may encounter with the employee?

4 ENGAGING EMPLOYEES THROUGH RECOGNITION

Engaging Employees Through Recognition

LEARN

Historically, recognition was given to employees based on their years of service with an organization through standard gifts at 5, 10, 15, 20, and 25+ years. In today's performance based work environments, the reasons for recognition have expanded in scope, as organizations realize that recognition should not only acknowledge *past* performance, but also should encourage *future* performance. Recognition programs are designed to increase the engagement levels of employees, so that they will be more likely to perform at higher levels. The challenge is that, as our partner TharpeRobbins (a leading USA recognition company) discussed with us, many organizations suffer from 'organizational inertia'. Organizations still struggle to understand how recognition programs can drive engagement and performance. Also, during times of austerity, organizations are reluctant to invest in recognition programs. However, the irony is that during tough economic times, recognition is increasingly important since organizations and leaders are asking employees to do more with less time, resources and guarantees. Being able to recognize employees, whether through a formalized recognition program or informally by leaders, is an essential leadership skill.

A recognition program is the process by which your organization acknowledges employees' performance contributions, considered to be above and beyond their role. Recognition is usually not given for meeting performance expectations, but for exceeding those expectations by either achieving superior results or by demonstrating organizational values. The objective of any recognition program is to increase engagement and performance. Rewards are the gifts received by the employee (e.g. jewellery, plaques, gift certificates, time-off, donation to a charity, etc.). All employee recognition programs are based on underlying principles of the psychological influences of motivation and the desire to perform. While we don't delve deep into these underlying theories, it is important to establish a baseline, so that you can evaluate your organization's recognition program. As a leader, you can either supplement your existing program with additional rewards, or initiate your own team recognition program with rewards that appeal to employees.

Employee Motivators: Extrinsic Rewards Through 'Carrots'

Many organizations have moved away from unstructured recognition programs based on subjective assessments by leaders, and are moving towards conditional recognition programs. Organizations and leaders detail exactly what conditions must be met in order for employees to be rewarded. For example, "if we finish the project on time, the team will go on a boat cruise." The underlying philosophy is that employees are motivated by extrinsic rewards. They need to know what rewards, termed 'carrots', are available if they perform well. Employees crave 'carrots'. They thrive when they have the tools needed to do a good job, when they have the opportunity to do what they do best, and when they receive recognition or praise for good work.[1] This approach is based on the belief that conditional recognition programs are the best way to achieve better results and to retain employees. 'Carrots' are dangled in front of employees to spur them on to reach company goals, to boost morale, to increase profit margins, to drive more business, and to recognize success. However, strict conditional recognition programs are not much different than any other incentive program. Many organizations acknowledge that conditional recognition may not have long lasting effects on engagement and performance. While these types of programs can definitely drive greater performance, they are often criticized for being narrow in focus, with only short-term effects.[2] The challenge with strict conditional recognition programs is that the rewards become normalized for employees, and are seen as part of the existing organization's total rewards program. The rewards no longer seem special and, instead, become something that is expected. Also, strict conditional reward programs often focus heavily on the results, not *how* employees achieve those results, and may not be flexible enough to recognize all positions within an organization (e.g. employees who are in non-revenue generating or administrative positions).

To respond to the challenges of strict conditional recognition programs, your organization should use broad criteria that employees must demonstrate in order to receive rewards. Organizations and leaders outline the values and behaviours they expect employees to demonstrate. Our client TharpeRobbins internally uses its values to reward employees. They broadly define 'courage' as meaning "when you put your soul into it, you set the standard." Taking risks without reprisal and making mistakes can all be behaviours of taking courage. Employees at all levels can demonstrate courage – from the warehouse, to the administration, to the leaders. TharpeRobbins is using recognition to help shape, influence and change its culture to one of increased engagement and performance.

Broad recognition criteria allow leaders to reach all roles and team members, as every role can demonstrate organizational values and desired behaviours.

Examples of recognition criteria that are conditional, but can be more broadly applied are:

- Exceeding expectations - exceptional quality of work
- Working hours required to get the job done
- Picking up a colleague's shift/responsibilities
- Working collaboratively within a cross-functional team
- Demonstrating organizational values in achieving goals
- Demonstrating a commitment to the organizational mission through day-to-day behaviours
- Building strong relationships with peers / colleagues / clients/stakeholders
- Getting up to speed quickly on a new project, role or job
- Taking risks and being innovative
- Saving the organization money
- Accepting accountability for errors/mistakes
- Identifying ways to individually contribute to the organizational goals and objectives

The challenge is that the less defined the criteria for conditional recognition, the more the program and the process are open to criticism. In a program where the criteria for recognition are broadly defined, it is very important for leaders to spend time with their teams discussing *how* employees can demonstrate the desired behaviours, given the operational environment. You have to be very transparent as to which types of behaviours will be recognized and why. Also, the process for recognition should be known and understood by all employees. When an employee receives recognition, the criteria for which s/he was recognized should be public, and be used as an example to other employees for how to achieve success. With broad conditional recognition programs, you are able to create an engaging work culture that drives individual and team performance.

Employees Motivators:
Intrinsic Rewards - Mastery, Purpose, Autonomy

Some researchers believe that the use of extrinsic motivators (carrots) through conditional recognition programs is based upon an antiquated concept of punishment and reward within the workplace.[3] To be truly successful, leaders must look beyond the basic motivational factors of rewarding and look at what intrinsically motivates employees. Intrinsic rewards mean that employees feel joy, engagement and empowerment from being able to perform at a high level. Employees are more motivated by the intrinsic satisfaction of having mastered a task, of being autonomous and finding purpose than any extrinsic reward they might receive. Proponents of this philosophy believe that extrinsic rewards (carrots) are only effective for tasks that have a clear set of rules and a simple outcome. However, in our modern age of knowledge-based work, which isn't narrowly focused and which requires more creativity and conceptualization, intrinsic rewards are more powerful in driving performance. Leaders should focus on workforce planning, role descriptions and task assignments that appeal to employees' intrinsic need for autonomy (the desire to direct our own lives), mastery (the desire to continually improve at something that matters) and purpose (the desire to do things for a purpose that is larger than oneself). In this approach, leaders might still recognize or highlight that employees have mastered a project or a task, but they do not necessarily provide a tangible reward. Essentially, the public recognition and acknowledgement is sufficient reward in and of itself.

It is perhaps utopian to think that we can create organizations where extrinsic rewards (carrots) that are based on conditions won't be necessary to drive performance. In most organizations, the majority of roles are clear and specific and do not require a high level of conceptualization and creativity. In those roles, extrinsic rewards will likely be effective in creating engagement (though it may be debatable how long engagement will remain high, when solely driven by extrinsic rewards). Also, it may not be realistic to believe that if employees' job tasks appealed to their intrinsic motivation of mastery and purpose that this is sufficient to drive high levels of performance. Even in these circumstances, many employees will still expect to be recognized for their achievements of having demonstrated mastery, autonomy or purpose in their work. However, it is interesting to consider the intrinsic motivation theory, as it relates to the generational perspective. It may be the case that the need and level of extrinsic rewards might vary depending on whether employees are focused on recognition within a career or within a job.

The most successful recognition program is a combination of both intrinsic and extrinsic rewards. The program must be dynamic, with leaders who are able to evaluate employees' motivators and identify which underlying theory resonates best for different employees in different situations. To be successful, you need to use your recognition program to extrinsically motivate employees with rewards that are meaningful to them. You also need to create a work environment that taps into intrinsic motivators by allowing employees to be as autonomous as possible, to learn and grow in order to achieve mastery of skills, and to understand the purposefulness of their work within the big picture. Regardless of the type of recognition, you need to acknowledge employee performance improves through on-going recognition over time. As our client TharpeRobbins coaches others 'it's not a sprint, it's a marathon'.

APPLY

You can evaluate your organization's recognition program, and identify what actions you can take to best recognize your employees, by:

Evaluating your organization's recognition program

- Is it designed on the principles of extrinsic rewards (carrots) within broad or strict conditions, or intrinsic rewards based on autonomy, mastery and purpose? How can you supplement your recognition program to encompass both theories of extrinsic and intrinsic motivation?

Understanding how your recognition system works

- Employees expect their leader to understand how to execute the organization's recognition program and to use it regularly. It is very disengaging if team members find out that a recognition program exists, but you choose not to use it. If your organization has created a recognition program, then it is incumbent upon you to use it to engage your employees.

Soliciting from employees how they would like to be rewarded

- Often, rewards can be free or have little cost associated, but can significantly drive performance and engagement levels. Identify all the ways that you can show employees that you value them as members of the team and that you appreciate their work.

Selecting the appropriate rewards for your employees

- If you have a choice as to which rewards you can give, ask employees what interests them and which rewards would be most appreciated and desired. Not every team member will find the same rewards interesting. While one employee might like a $25 dollar gift card to the movie theatre, another might enjoy a restaurant gift card, while yet another would prefer to donate the $25 to a charity.

Actively demonstrate that rewarding employees is important to you

- If your organization uses a point system that allows employees to collect points towards a certain reward item, ask employees what they are saving up for. Then, the next time they receive points, congratulate them on getting one step closer to their desired reward. This shows that you are paying attention and that you care about the employee's continued engagement.

Differentiating and balancing individual recognition and team recognition

- Many employees would like the whole team, or a sub-group who worked on a project, to receive acknowledgement. Team recognition can also lead to team building, which strengthens your team dynamics and workplace culture. Encourage the team to identify a group reward that they can all share in. If it's an experience, like dinner out or an activity together, it will strengthen team relationships and improve collaboration.

Involving others in the process of recognition

- It's important to encourage team members to recognize each other for a job well done, for more senior leaders to be aware when you are recognizing an employee, and for employees to be able to give you a pat on the back for a job well done as a leader.

UPGRADE

When leading a multigenerational team, it is important to understand each generation's expectations and desires for recognition. While there are unique generational preferences, it is possible that members of different generations may want the same reward, and certainly every generation desires recognition. However, by paying attention to how each generation adds a new dimension to the expectation of being recognized, it provides you with insights into how recognition programs should be designed and executed.

Gen Xers and Gen Ys tend to view their employment relationship as a transactional investment rather than a longer term investment within a full career, which is the view often held by Baby

Boomers and Traditionalists. This means that the concept of extrinsic vs. intrinsic rewards may have to be evaluated differently between younger and experienced employees.

For many Traditionalist employees, recognition was something that they experienced on rare occasions. Other than length of service rewards, which often weren't given until an employee reached 10+ years with an organization, recognition was not expected on a consistent basis. Today, for many Traditionalists, a pat on the back or a 'good job' comment at a team meeting is much appreciated. Many in this cohort have the mindset that they are being paid to do their job, which is recognition enough.

Baby Boomers understand that recognition is an important mechanism to differentiate employees. In particular, 'star' employees are centered out for their exceptional contributions. Similar to Traditionalists, recognition was not a frequent occurrence for many Baby Boomers and was usually based on tenure within the organization and/or stages within their career. It is important for this cohort to have recognition conducted in public, in front of peers and other leaders, so as to communicate their value and importance to the team and organization. Recognition programs can also be used as a mechanism to spur on competition between employees and to encourage others to work harder and achieve greater results. Because of this generation's desire to be acknowledged by senior leaders, items of recognition that highlight status within the organization are well appreciated.

Gen Xers were the first generation to expect recognition as a normal part of the employment experience. They believe that if they are doing an exceptional job, they should be recognized for going above and beyond in their role. Otherwise, if there aren't rewards, they will often be satisfied to just remain a 'good' employee and won't strive to be 'great'. They believe that recognition is possible in every role, at every level, in every organization, regardless of the stage within their career. The rewards that appeal to this cohort must have value to them at an individual level, and not just be an item that the organization wants to give. Gen Xers also bring to the workplace a desire to recognize peers for doing a great job, or demonstrating organizational values. Because Gen Xers primarily focus on achieving results, they are quick to acknowledge team members who have helped them (and the team) achieve results needed for success.

Gen Ys have grown up in a world where they have been recognized constantly, often for just participating and not necessarily achieving results. In extra-curricular activities, such as sport teams, everyone gets a trophy. In the classroom, each student is recognized for having a unique talent. This generation has brought into the workplace an expectation that recognition should happen frequently, for a variety of reasons, and occur at the team level, not just the individual level. Rewards should be personalized and unique to each employee. Since this generation has often been given a lot of material items, the rewards provided need to be creative, unique, hip or trendy. Gen Ys not only want to be able to recognize their peers, but also expect that they can evaluate and nominate you (or other leaders) within the organization for strong leadership skills.

Generational Reward Items

Different generational cohorts are drawn to different types of rewards. Our client, Starwood Properties, has recognized this fact. They conduct a yearly survey to understand what's working and what's not within its recognition program and which rewards are most valuable to employees. By walking 'the floor to solicit face to face feedback,' Starwood leaders learned that younger associates were tired of the same old recognition/service programs that still resonate well with experienced generations. The Starwood team realised that the younger generations are unique and simply want different rewards to motivate them.

Extrinsic vs. Intrinsic Rewards

Baby Boomers may not be recognized within every job they hold, but they seek to build their recognition profile over their entire career. They may accept roles and jobs that do not intrinsically motivate them, because they have a longer term, bigger picture view of striving for recognition within their career. Since they view the concept of a career more 'holistically' than the younger generations, they accept that they may have to be satisfied with non-engaging work, until they can reach the next level. For many Baby Boomers, as they wind down their careers, the desire for extrinsic recognition wanes. Having already achieved the highest peak possible, they are more content with finding roles that provide intrinsic recognition, as evidenced by the number of Baby Boomers who leave the for-profit world to do work they feel is more meaningful / purposeful in the not-for-profit space.

The situation is different for the younger generations. They expect to be intrinsically rewarded in every role. They are less inclined to accept or stay in a role, unless they can achieve mastery, purpose, and autonomy. Many Gen Xers and Gen Ys are engaged and satisfied when they have intrinsic rewards, since they are focused on developing professional skill sets, learning, growing, and getting results. A challenging work assignment is a reward to younger employees since it allows them to develop mastery and connect with the purposefulness of their work. Their desire for extrinsic recognition grows as they become less and less engaged. For a Gen Xer, if the primary motivator becomes solely extrinsic recognition, then chances are that the employee is headed towards the end of his/her tenure with your organization. A distinction between Gen Xers and Gen Ys is that Gen Ys have a higher expectation of both intrinsic and extrinsic reward. They expect that their work will intrinsically motivate them but, in addition to the rewards or mastery, purpose and autonomy, they also expect extrinsic rewards that are of high value to them. This cohort has grown up in a world where they have received ribbons, trophies and banners for everything, from participating in sports, to attending school, to getting their homework done. They didn't have authority figures tell them that 'doing a good job is reward enough.'

So, if the goal is to increase employee engagement and deliver business results, the expectations of recognition by the four generations need to be met, or managed, by a program that is comprehensive and flexible enough to address diverse needs. What appeals and motivates one generation may not appeal and motivate another. You have to be practical by evaluating what is important to your employees, and by consistently executing recognition that will engage them to high performance.

EXECUTE

Use this tool to guide you through recognizing your employees. Recognition should become an ingrained leadership behaviour that you demonstrate consistently.

1. Describe what employee behaviours you value as a leader? List at least three.

2. How do these behaviours align with the expectations of your organization's recognition program (results, values)?

3. Who were the last three employees that you recognized and why? List how they demonstrated desired behaviours and values.

4. Discuss at your next team meeting, the organization's recognition program. Prepare in advance:
   - The behaviours and values that are recognized
   - How decisions are made
   - Who is eligible to receive a reward? Who can give recognition? (E.g. Can employees recognize each other? Can employees recognize another leader?)

5. How does your organization use extrinsic rewards? If your organization uses a point system for rewards, do you know what types of rewards are meaningful to each employee?

6. If your organization does not use a point system, solicit employee input via a survey or by providing a list of options where employees can rank their preferences.

7. When an employee has mastered a new skill, has created purpose or has demonstrated autonomy, how will you acknowledge that achievement?

5 EMPOWERING EMPLOYEES THROUGH EFFECTIVE DELEGATION

Empowering Employees Through Effective Delegation

LEARN

Empowerment and delegation – simple terms, yet difficult to execute. One of the most effective ways to empower employees is *through* delegation. However, leaders often don't delegate at all, or they struggle with how to do it. The reluctance to delegate is typically based on various professional fears, and rigid beliefs of what it means to be efficient and perfect in completing tasks. In addition, while leaders talk about empowering their employees, many would state that they themselves do not feel empowered. The problem is that you can't become a high-performing leader, unless you empower your employees to assume greater responsibility through well-coordinated delegation. Delegation is a necessary business skill. With resource constraints, you cannot be highly productive if you do everything yourself, or if you micromanage tasks to completion. Being able to effectively delegate allows you to take on other activities/projects and allows you to focus on more strategic responsibilities. The more you delegate, the more empowered your employees will be. The feeling of empowerment is a significant contributor to increasing employee engagement levels.

The reason why empowerment can be realised through effective delegation is that the definitions of empowerment inherently possess the factors central to delegation.

Empowerment can be defined as:

> *The process of releasing the full potential of employees in order for them to take on greater responsibility and authority in the decision-making process, and providing the resources for this process to occur.*[1]
>
> *To empower someone implies that you also provide them with skills, information, authority, and resources to carry out their responsibilities.*[2]
>
> *All empowerment must involve meaningful tasks, competence, and self-determination.*[3]

While the definitions seem simple, they are more easily conceptualized than executed. Employees often feel as "though they do not have the support or resources to actually become empowered."[4] Also employees are often unclear as to what empowerment means in tangible terms. Commonly, they equate it to a *feeling* of freedom provided by leaders, rather than specific actions taken by their leaders. Through effective delegation, you will be able to demonstrate that you are empowering your employees.

By all definitions, the act of empowering includes:

- Increasing employee accountabilities
- Supporting employees to make decisions
- Allowing employees to be self-directed

Each of these elements is achieved through effective delegation. To measure and quantify empowerment is to measure whether or not you have effectively delegated. Therefore, empowerment is measurable, quantifiable and definable. It is not intangible; rather, it is a concrete process of leadership through effective delegation.

Principles of Effective Delegation

Delegation is not about getting rid of all the activities that you are too busy to complete, or that you dislike. It is about giving employees the accountability to make the right decisions, to change the process, and to be the owner of the task or project.

Effective delegation means:

- Identifying what tasks, activities or projects to delegate
- Communicating thoroughly the expectations and parameters
- Ensuring that all resources are available
- Building trust by being a facilitative manager
- Clearing obstacles for employees to ensure success

It is important that you create a positive, supportive team culture, where colleagues are encouraged to help each other. Delegation is most successful when there is a win-win outcome — key tasks, activities or projects are re-assigned appropriately, and employees build new skills or achieve new results by taking on greater accountability.

Delegation is not just pushing work down. When you are delegating, you are consulting and developing as well as assigning work. Open communication is vital, and success depends ultimately on the communication skills of the manager and the employee and on the quality of their relationship. When there is a lack of trust on either side, or poor communication between them, the required under-standing and motivation are unlikely to be there.[5]

Objections to Delegating

Since delegation creates employee empowerment, why don't more leaders do it? There are several objections that leaders use to defend why they don't delegate. However, there are equally valid responses to these objections, which also highlight the benefits of delegating.[6]

Objection / Cost	Response / Benefit
It takes too much time	Initially you spend more time invested in planning, preparing, explaining, training, coaching, and monitoring the delegated work than you would by just doing it yourself. However, this does not hold true after the employee is successfully accountable for the task.
I should do it myself	As a leader, you are responsible for resource management. Are you really the best resource to complete that task, activity, or project?
I can do it better and faster	With experience, other employees can learn to do it as well and as quickly as you can, freeing up your time for higher-priority activities.

Objection / Cost	Response / Benefit
If it's not done right, I'll just have to do it over.	There are steps you can follow to reduce or minimize the risk of errors. If you communicate appropriately, with regular check-ins, errors can be avoided or solved early.
I'd rather do it myself.	You need to let go of certain work that you enjoy to concentrate on things that only you can accomplish.
If I let someone else do it, I'll lose control.	Giving employees authority to complete tasks and make certain decisions is not abdicating. You still share responsibility for accomplishing the work and achieving success.
I don't have anyone to delegate to.	A primary reason for delegating is to help others learn new skills.
Everyone is already too busy.	Delegating is not dumping. It's providing opportunities, as long you provide employees with enough time to do the work.
If people learn my job, I'll be out of work.	Leaders who can successfully get work done through others and expand others' competencies are more valuable to the organization.

Many of these objections are based on professional fears that delegating could have a negative impact on operational results or leaders' careers. For example, leaders fear: that they won't be seen as competent, because others are doing the work; that they will be replaced; and that if something goes wrong, it will impact their reputation. These fears are generally unfounded and can be managed through effective delegation. The benefits of effectively delegating far outweigh the risks. Employees may make mistakes when they first take over a new project or task, just as you may make mistakes in executing the principles of effective delegation. What's critical is that you view those mistakes as a valuable part of the learning curve for both yourself and the employee.

The key point is that, if we want employees to take the risk of being accountable in making important decisions, they must feel they can trust management and the organizational systems. In hierarchical organizations, compliance is often rewarded more than good judgment. Unless this relationship changes, talk of empowerment will be perceived as an organizational lie. People will be wondering, 'What will happen if I make a bad decision, but make it in good faith and with my best effort?' If people fear the consequences (that is, if they do not trust the leadership), then they will not be willing to take the risk to make business decisions. It is safer not to act and to just let someone else make those decisions— hence, no empowerment occurs.[7]

Thus, to be an effective delegator, it is important that you assess your risk tolerance. Do not ask employees to take greater risk than you or your organizational culture supports. Unless you are prepared to stand behind your employees with managerial courage when they make mistakes, don't ask them to do something you wouldn't do. Also, you may be surprised at how open senior leaders are to you increasing the responsibilities of your team through delegation. Your own inclination to limit delegation may actually be more conservative than what your organizational culture desires. This assessment gap could be a result of a discrepancy between your fears of delegation and your assessment of your organization's risk tolerance. Often leaders say that they can't delegate certain responsibilities; however, that is not an operational reality, but rather a professional fear.

Benefits

Many leaders loathe the idea of delegation because they are perfectionists, control-centered, sceptics, 'gun-shy' or just uncomfortable with the unexpected. Leaders must get over these negative characteristics, if they are to become 'agile' managers.[8] The notion of agility links to your ability to become more strategic in your work. Effective delegation allows you to rise above monitoring the minutiae, day-to-day tasks, to a broader view of how the team's work links to your own operational goals. It allows you to focus on tasks where you can add more value, based on your level of expertise. The outcome is that you are managing goals and results, rather than tactics. Also, effective delegation allows your organization's resources to be managed efficiently. Since people are a fundamental and costly resource in every organization, you have an obligation to manage those resources efficiently. Finally, effective delegation can reduce your stress levels, because you have empowered employees to take accountability for their work.

There are also benefits for employees. Effective delegation raises their level of engagement because you:

- Demonstrate that you trust employees to use their knowledge and judgement in a way that is consistent with your expectations and the organization's values to reach goals
- Satisfy employee ego and self-esteem needs
- Allow employees to grow within their present jobs

APPLY

To demonstrate the principles of effective delegation, you must take the following actions:

Rate your own comfort level with delegation

- How often do you delegate? Why do or don't you do it? When delegating, do you achieve positive results? If yes, why? If no, why not? Until you understand your own inclination and ability to effectively delegate, you won't be able to set employees up for success.

Start delegating right away

- This can be done even with new employees, in incremental steps. Determine which pieces of work can be delegated. These pieces should be whole tasks, self-contained activities, projects or responsibilities and not just transactional tasks. Our client, Shoppers Drug Mart, emphasizes that leaders need to rethink the way they perceive new employees. Rather than viewing them as too inexperienced to take on more meaningful work, they should recognize that new entrants to the workforce often have a lot of knowledge and have learned a lot of skills that the existing workforce may not possess (e.g. technological, multi-tasking, approaches to building solutions, diversity).

Build up employees' responsibilities over time

- First, assign responsibilities that have a high likelihood for success and less risk, and then increase to responsibilities that require greater decision-making and analytic reasoning skills with a higher chance of error. As employees come to understand your thinking, to learn your approach, to become more familiar with the organizational culture and operational realities, they will be more likely to make the right decisions, and achieve the desired results. However, this takes time.

Be clear

- Describe in detail how tasks, activities or projects fit into the bigger picture, and your expectations and standards (quality, timelines, stakeholder involvement, resources etc.).

Provide employees with the resources required to be successful

- Those may include: enough time to complete the project; finances; access to other stakeholders; technology; training; etc.

Leave employees alone

- Give employees the space and time to complete tasks independently. Set up regular status up-dates and touch point meetings to help remove barriers, to act as a sounding board, and to provide coaching. It is important that you do not hover, micromanage, or second guess every decision made by employees. Focus more on the results than on the process. This will demonstrate that you trust your employees' judgements and abilities.

Evaluate the results

- Collaboratively review the results of each newly delegated project. What did they do well? What do they need to do differently next time? This process starts to build knowledge and competency of how to repeat, replicate and complete projects appropriately in the future with less guidance from you.

Reward success

- Acknowledge and recognize when a project has been completed well, especially something newly delegated. Ask employees to share with you what new skills or competencies they have learned, so that you can reinforce the new learning and reward future application.

UPGRADE

Delegation is difficult to execute for many leaders, regardless of generation, since it is often perceived as losing control. In a Traditionalist work environment, delegation is seen as a weakness. The concept of empowerment is not part of leaders' vernacular. In this environment, an effective leader should have control over all matters related to his/her team, and should be the ultimate decision maker. Delegation was potentially risky for a leader. If the work didn't get done properly or on time, s/he was still held fully accountable. In this type of risk-adverse work environment, mistakes are not tolerated and the fear of failure is great. For Traditionalists to be comfortable delegating, they must believe they have the support of their senior leaders and that small project errors are acceptable during the transition period.

Baby Boomers also experienced this type of rigid environment as employees, and, in some industries and sectors, continue to experience it. Our client, Shoppers Drug Mart, has noticed that Baby Boomers sometimes struggle with relinquishing control and delegating because of their own historical work experiences. They are hesitant to delegate, because they worry about their own reputations. Given the highly competitive work environment for Baby Boomers, a mistake in delegation could mean losing a promotion, or not getting assigned to the next project. Delegation might not feel comfortable, because losing control of the details might be perceived as a decrease in their 'work-value'. The concern is 'if someone else knows how to implement the process, modifies it, or is in charge of making decisions, what value do I have?' For Baby Boomer leaders, it's important that they realize that delegation allows them to take on even greater responsibilities that focus on their strengths and their desires to add value to the organization.

Gen Xers may be more inclined to delegate, especially tasks or projects that they feel do not add value to their professional portfolio or skills repertoire. They, generally, recognize that the more employees can do, the greater likelihood of achieving team results. Because Gen Xers dislike being micromanaged themselves, they may be inclined to not give sufficient background information or detailed instructions to employees when handing over responsibilities. While this cohort is fundamentally interested in setting up their employees for success, they often take a 'sink or swim' approach when delegating projects. This is intended to be a sign of respect by Gen X leaders, since they believe that by waiting for employees to come and ask questions, rather than micromanaging how things get done, they are demonstrating trust in employees' abilities. To be effective delegators, Gen Xers need to focus on providing the required tools for employees to succeed and to focus on providing the right level of coaching.

Gen Y employees are open to being delegated to. Shoppers Drug Mart observes that there's a real desire for empowerment by Gen Y: "When they enter the workplace, that's one of the things they place value on. For them it's not about hierarchies, but rather about having accountability and responsibility within the job role." They are accustomed to a world of hyper collaboration, where team members share responsibilities. However, as leaders, Gen Ys may avoid delegating tasks or responsibilities, if they know the employee won't be thrilled with the added responsibility, since they often have a strong personal relationship with employees. They are not accustomed to asking others to do things that they don't want to do, so they may initially worry about hurting employees' feelings. Their biggest challenge, though, may actually be that many Gen Ys don't understand the hierarchical nature of most organizational cultures, and therefore do not understand why they cannot delegate 'up' to more senior people. We've had many leaders share with us how astonished they are when Gen Ys have said to them 'I can't get this done right now, why don't you do it?' Gen Ys are effective delegators, if they leverage the trust they have built with their teams by openly sharing how increased responsibilities benefits employees, the team, and the organization.

EXECUTE

n-gen uses a three-step process to delegating greater responsibilities to team members. It includes: learning; owning the execution; and improving on the process/task.

STEP 1 - LEARN IT

Employees actively listen and proactively ask questions about the task, activity, or project.

- The employee is involved in all interactions, including listening in on calls, reading all emails sent to stakeholders, attending all meetings. Essentially, s/he is shadowing the owner of the task.

- After each interaction, the leader conducts a quick discussion/debrief to explain details that might not be obvious: who the stakeholder is; why a certain approach was taken; what the interaction has to do with the task, activity or project; how it all links to operational goals (e.g. business development, administration, research, finance, marketing); what the next steps are.

- The employee takes notes during each interaction, and asks the leader questions.

Employees are accountable to understand the who, what, why, how and when for the assigned task/activity/project.

STEP 2 - OWN IT

Employees implement the task/activity/project with minimal supervision and few mistakes.

- The employee takes over the task, activity or project with close supervision at first. The leader listens, but does not initiate or lead interactions, is cc'd on all emails, and attends meetings as the support person or subject matter expert.

- Debriefs continue after each interaction that the employee leads, to provide coaching and to address any errors made.

- As the employee either proactively states that s/he is ready, or the leader decides the employee is ready, the leader gradually drops out of interactions (calls, meetings, emails). This is a critical stage because leaders must trust that their employees are ready to 'fly solo'. Ensure through open conversations with the employee that s/he is ready. Does s/he need more coaching, shadowing or learning?

- Owning it means that the employee is responsible for providing status updates, alerting the leader to any challenges or impending risks.

Employees are accountable for the successful execution of the task, activity or project.

STEP 3 – IMPROVE IT

Employees use creativity and innovation to improve the task, activity or project.

- If an employee faces challenges, s/he proactively offers solutions for how to overcome them.

- The employee proactively presents suggestions and ideas for improvement. As the employee is working within the new responsibility, s/he should identify ways to improve the task, activity, project. For example, this could mean a new reporting tool, a way to save money, cutting steps in a process for faster completion, etc.

- Depending on the nature of the responsibility, the employee may be required to present suggested improvements quarterly, bi-yearly or yearly. It may be the case that major improvements can't be made, but this activity encourages the employee to look at his/her responsibilities proactively with a sense of ownership towards making positive changes.

- Leaders act as a check-and-balance to ensure that suggested improvements align to organizational and team goals, strategies, and policies. Leaders should say 'yes' more frequently than 'no' to suggested improvements, in order to encourage on-going innovation and creativity. If there are barriers to implementing recommended improvements, leaders are responsible to remove those barriers, or to coordinate with other stakeholders to assess possible implementation plans.

Employees are accountable to ensure that their operational responsibilities are being performed at the highest level.

6

LEADING VIRTUAL TEAMS

Leading Virtual Teams

LEARN

As a result of globalization, outsourcing and joint ventures, the creation of virtual teams requires stronger collaboration skills than ever before. Global working groups bring with them a series of strengths and challenges. Small and mid-sized organizations are giving employees more flexibility to work from home or on the road, which translates into less face to face time and a greater need to collaborate using technology. With a strong shift towards knowledge and information based organizations, employees can complete their work anytime, anywhere. Companies such as Google and Sun Microsystems estimate that at least 50% of their employees work on virtual teams at any given time.[1]

Regardless if team members are from across the globe, or just across the same city, virtual teams are a collection of employees who:

- Are interdependent in their tasks
- Have shared common goals and responsibilities for outcomes
- Are geographically disperse
- Are electronically dependent
- Are dynamic or comprise diverse members
- Are self-reliant and self-motivated
- Are viewed by themselves (and others) to be an intact unit

Virtual teams often have the added complexity of needing to manage time zone differences, language barriers and cultural differences. Mobile workers are available and accountable anywhere and anytime. The mobile workforce may be located at home or on the road, or it may simply be moving within your own corporate settings. Mobile workers perform critical jobs for an organization, using secure Internet connections, collaborating from near to as far as anywhere on the globe you can imagine, using the most appropriate hardware and software needed to get the work done. The most effective mobile workforces have the support and leadership of management, who provide both the technological and organizational tools to assure success.[2] Our client, Cisco, to which we provide global training to managers and Gen Ys, have identified that 85% of their employees regularly work from home or on the road, with 48% of work being done off-hours.

Advantages

It is important to recognize that there are several advantages to establishing virtual teams and managing them well, even though much is written about the challenges. As organizations adopt more flexible work arrangements, there are strategic and bottom-line improvements, such as increased employee engagement, productivity, attraction, retention, and reduced health-care costs.[3] In addition, by leveraging technology to conduct team meetings, travel costs are significantly reduced. At Cisco, we have discovered that they achieved a 90% cost savings by hosting their global annual sales conference online using high-definition video and a slew of other Cisco products.

Our client, Chevron, states that the benefits of virtual teams are two-fold. Firstly, the organization is able to retain valuable subject matter experts (when providing remote work options to semi-retired Baby Boomers), and is able to use them to add value to the project. Secondly, employees benefit by having the flexibility to manage their own schedules, continue to do work they enjoy, and increase their engagement levels.

Barriers and Challenges

There are several challenges virtual teams face, that can have a significant impact on performance and engagement levels.

Challenges include:

- Lack of clear goals and direction
- Lack of clear roles and responsibilities
- Feelings of isolation and disconnection
- Difficulty cultivating trust and collaboration among team members
- Cross-cultural communication barriers
- Lack of resources
- Difficulty coordinating over various time zones
- Shifting team and organizational priorities
- Difficulty managing poor performance

High Performing Virtual Teams

Teams that excel at working in a virtual environment do so by focusing on three areas:

1. **Process**

    - Clearly understand and commit to a common goal
    - Have clearly defined roles
    - Communicate frequently
    - Share information freely
    - Meet virtually at least once a week
    - Leverage dynamic collaborative technologies to brainstorm and problem solve
    - Document reliable, repeatable work processes
    - Strongly monitor and evaluate tasks completed
    - Hire the right people who will succeed in a virtual environment

2. **People**

    - Share an enthusiasm for working together
    - Trust each other
    - Respect diversity
    - Collaborate regularly to complete tasks
    - Empower team members to make decisions
    - Support each other to achieve goals

3. Performance

- Are results oriented
- Maximize individual strengths
- Are creative, innovative and flexible
- Celebrate successes
- Have a leader who motivates and engages all

The two most important characteristics of high performing virtual teams are trust and communication. Trust is achieved by creating a safe environment where employees can openly express feelings, speak up, and take risks. Through small daily interactions, a trusting environment is created. It is more challenging to build trust with someone that you may not see face to face or with whom you don't share the same native language or culture. Trust is required to achieve collaboration and, therefore, is a critical focus. Trust is comprised of four components: credibility; reliability; intimacy; and self-orientation.

Communication is central to all business interactions. However, it is particularly important for virtual teams. When working in the same location, employees tend to communicate more frequently and develop closer and more positive interpersonal relationships through frequent, informal interactions. Virtual teams must try to mimic that environment since, by default, the lack of proximity to each other decreases closeness between group members. Our client, Chevron, manages their virtual teams by leveraging collaborative tools, such as video conferencing, to ensure teams connect via telepresence on a regular basis. This provides a close replica of a face to face meeting. In addition, they focus on improving internal communication, since written communication (e.g. emails) can be interpreted either positively or negatively depending on the reader, and therefore, it is important to recognize when a phone call or face to face meeting is needed.

APPLY

Overall, what it takes to effectively manage a virtual team isn't all that different from what is required to lead in any other circumstance. However, leaders who aren't strong people managers will struggle to be able to engage, motivate and empower virtual employees. The business skills of management are much more critical to success when leading a virtual team, than they are when leading a team that is co-located.

Chevron states that "The first challenge for any leader is that their leadership style has to look different – not necessarily has to change, however, it must employ creativity in how they are going to adapt their leadership style to a virtual environment." There are several actions you can take to effectively manage virtual or remote employees. The first is being aware of what mobile employees need and expect from you.

Virtual teams want a leader that:

- Coordinates rather than controls
- Is honest and trustworthy
- Is accessible and responsive
- Gives feedback instead of advice
- Is caring and concerned for employees' well-being
- Builds a sense of team spirit
- Respects all employees
- Trusts and empowers employees to get the work done

Therefore, the top five leadership behaviours to effectively lead a virtual team are:

1. **Defining and clarifying** – establish strategy, vision and team goals

2. **Communicating** – establish on-going dialogue using a range of mediums

3. **Coaching** – assess performance and providing learning support for success

4. **Accountability** – accept shared accountability for the team's success

5. **Caring** – build a personal relationship with team members and foster collaboration

Keep in mind that when leading a global team, you will also need to pay special attention to:

Cultural differences: A misunderstanding of different cultural norms and an absence of face to face time can significantly impact levels of trust. Differing holiday schedules can also impede collaboration.

Local HR policies: Laws and policies will differ.

Budget: Build in costs for at least one face-to-face meeting to build rapport.

Time zones: Don't schedule meetings at times that are only convenient for you or team members in your time zone. Rotate meeting times to be respectful to all.

UPGRADE

For Traditionalists, they got up each morning and went to work. This meant a physical, brick and mortar location. There were few, if any, virtual employees and work wasn't completed at home. When you were at the office, you worked. When you left, the work was also left behind. So, for Traditionalist leaders who are now managing virtual or global teams, their management style must adjust. The typical structure used to measure performance, such as observing someone at their desk, coming in and leaving on time, and adhering to rules and policies, won't work. Instead, Traditionalists must focus on the outcomes and results. If Traditionalist employees are expected to work remotely and contribute to a virtual team, they will expect a lot of direction setting by you as a leader. Be clear about accountabilities, with whom they should collaborate and how, and how you will measure success. Since they won't be physically able to demonstrate their dedication and hard work, you can expect to receive regular status up-dates from Traditionalist employees on what tasks they have completed.

As one Baby Boomer manager said in our leadership workshop: "Not having to come into the office and being able to work from home is a privilege that must be earned; it is not an automatic right." This mindset is shared by many leaders who believe that only high performers should be allowed to work remotely as a reward. With the construction of global, virtual teams this work style is no longer a luxury, but a necessity. Baby Boomer employees who are part of virtual teams want to build credibility to ensure they are well positioned in the team and that they can add value. They may struggle with building strong relationships, if there is no ability to meet face to face. The use of highly interactive technology is important to ensure a more engaging experience with team members.

Many Baby Boomers welcome the ability to work on a virtual team due to the flexibility and enhanced work-life balance that can be achieved.

Gen Xers are well positioned to excel as virtual team members. Given this generation's strong independence, self-reliance on achieving outcomes, and focus on results, Gen Xers thrive in an environment where they can work independently and collaborate using technology when needed. Chevron has found younger employees (Gen X & Y) are more easily adaptable to virtual team environments and desire this type of work arrangement. Gen Xers expect all team members to be competent in completing their individual tasks, but are quick to help their colleagues when everyone is clear on how working together will achieve the team's goal. Gen Xers who lead virtual teams are often very effective, because they adopt a results-based approach and don't place an emphasis on how or when work is completed, as long as the outcome is delivered on time and to the right standards. One area that Gen X leaders may struggle with is spending sufficient time building a strong relationship with team members, and in factoring in time and money for social team discussions and events that are not tied to achieving business results.

Gen Ys have participated in virtual teams for years, prior to working for your organization. They have been gaming with friends around the world, they have been solving problems with their classmates online through group discussions, they have been forming relationships and staying connected with others using social media, even if they have never met face-to-face. Gen Ys are comfortable using technology to collaborate. However, where this cohort may struggle initially, when joining a virtual team, is working independently, with little social interaction. This lack of connection can be a cause for disengagement, as they have a strong desire to feel as though they are a part of the team. Be prepared to receive feedback and suggestions from Gen Y virtual team members on how technology can be better leveraged to increase collaboration.

In addition, Gen Ys desire a lot of feedback and coaching on their performance, so they expect to be given clear direction on what to do and comprehensive feedback on how well they performed. This can be a challenge for leaders of virtual teams since it is difficult to assess day to day activities. It is important to involve others (from the local area if possible) and/or colleagues and customers to gather input on how well Gen Y employees are performing. In addition, your ability to connect what they do to big picture goals is important in empowering this cohort to take ownership and accountability for their contributions to a project. Gen Ys, who are now beginning to lead virtual teams, are blending their personal and professional lives. They are often becoming friends with their team members on Facebook, and are intertwining personal and professional conversations. They are strong online collaborators, but may struggle with how to engage employees who are more experienced in age than them, especially if the experienced employees aren't as comfortable or interested in using online tools as their primary method of communication.

EXECUTE

Use the charts below to help you identify the goals and actions you can take to demonstrate the top five leadership behaviours required to successfully lead a virtual team.

Defining & clarifying

Goals	Actions
▪ Develop the mission, strategy and vision of the team ▪ Link each project/task to the goals of the department/organization ▪ Clarify responsibilities	▪ Communicate the team's common goal ▪ Outline accountabilities of all team members ▪ Outline performance expectations (results, competencies, behaviours, timelines)

Communication

Goals	Actions
<ul><li>Create on-going dialogue</li><li>Match the right technology to the task</li><li>Establish communication protocols</li></ul>	<ul><li>Use telephone, email, video-conferencing, audio-conferencing, webex, live chat, team blogs, social media sites etc. to stay connected to the team and encourage communication across team members</li><li>Build a 'cyber café' or virtual space, using your intranet or a social media site to allow team members to stay in touch, talk informally, and connect on a more personal level</li><li>Agree on communication practices – who to keep in the loop, how frequently project status up-dates will occur, the need for clear and concise language in emails, etc.</li></ul>

Coaching

Goals	Actions
<ul><li>Assess performance and provide learning support for success</li><li>Support team members to achieve goals</li></ul>	<ul><li>Conduct regular formal assessments (ideally 1x/quarter)</li><li>Provide frequent and ongoing informal feedback</li><li>Develop performance improvement plans that may involve resources at the employee's location</li><li>Review performance expectations (results, competencies, behaviours, timelines, responsibilities)</li><li>Develop methods for sharing best practices with other team members</li></ul>

Accountability

Goals	Actions
■ Demonstrate shared accountability for the team's success ■ Remove corporate and technological roadblocks ■ Serve as a role model	■ Focus on results and outcomes, not time ■ Share the problem, but look to the team to create solutions ■ Provide training on how to overcome conflict so employees will address issues head-on instead of avoiding them ■ Provide cross-cultural training, if required, to improve cultural sensitivity ■ Attend all scheduled meetings ■ Avoid re-scheduling team meetings ■ Share information on your work goals ■ Keep your promises by completing your deliverables to team members

Caring

Goals	Actions
▪ Know your team members well on a personal and professional level	▪ Send weekly/monthly updates of personal stories from across the team
▪ Foster an environment of collaboration	▪ Build a strong personal relationship with each team member
▪ Build a sense of community	▪ Allow team members to post family news and photos on the team virtual site
▪ Celebrate successes	▪ Host annual team building sessions
	▪ Find other leaders that are in the same location as virtual team members and ask them to engage in group events
	▪ Perform virtual recognition to celebrate achievements and acknowledge high performance
	▪ Provide individual and team rewards

7 MANAGING EXPERIENCED EMPLOYEES

Managing Experienced Employees: Leadership Skills for Gen X and Gen Y

LEARN

For the first time in working history, younger generations are managing older generations in the workplace. In fact, it is becoming increasingly common for Gen Xers and Gen Ys to be managing employees from the Baby Boomer and Traditionalist generations. More and more Baby Boomers are delaying retirement, because they are living longer, are healthier, are enjoying working and, in many cases, can't afford to retire. In addition, many healthy Traditionalists have decided to re-enter the workforce, even if only on a part-time basis. It used to be the case that leaders were older than their employees, because they had more knowledge and experience. Today, the percentage of post-secondary graduates is higher. Younger employees are exposed to a lot more information (in our 24/7 internet world) and skill-building experiences while growing up than were previous generations. Thus, they enter into the workplace with significant competencies and knowledge which often allows them to leap frog over the older generations into leadership positions earlier in their careers.

"*As generations continue to mix in the workplace, many older workers are reporting to younger bosses. A new CareerBuilder survey finds that 43 percent of workers ages 35 and older said they currently work for someone younger than them. Breaking down age groups, more than half (53 percent) of workers ages 45 and up said they have a boss younger than them, followed by 69 percent of workers ages 55 and up.*"[1]

This new workplace reality, where younger leaders manage more experienced employees (those older in age and with more years of experience), brings with it interesting dynamics. While Baby Boomers and Traditionalists often are confused about how to manage Gen X and Gen Y employees, younger leaders are not always confident that they manage the older generations effectively either. The root of the issue is that, while the four generations may use the same language in the workplace, they actually define words and concepts differently. Moreover, these varying definitions actually result in varying behaviours. These differing definitions and behaviours are where the confusion, the mis-steps, and misunderstandings are rooted. When it comes to managing experienced employees, you must be aware that there are essentially five fundamental differences in the way work is approached.

Five Fundamental Differences Between the Generations

1. Work style

Perhaps the most obvious difference between the generations is how the work day is structured. Gen Xers and Gen Ys adopt a very flexible and fluid work style. They are comfortable with greater ambiguity in the flow of their work day. They expect to control how and where they get work done. They seek the greatest amount of flexibility in order to be able to blend both work and life responsibilities within their day. In interviewing our client, Clorox, they highlighted that the younger generations have a different way of approaching work, which can be frustrating for some older workers. For example, younger managers work from home on a regular basis and run personal errands during work hours. For Gen Xers and Gen Ys, activities such as going to the bank, picking up dry cleaning, and checking their social networking sites do not necessarily have to be relegated to non-work hours. They work where and when it best suits them, while ensuring that they achieve their results, because *how* and *when* work is done is not the critical factor. They often view the Traditionalists' insistence on following policies and Baby Boomers' adherence to processes and procedures as potentially inefficient and non-productive. But younger leaders need to realise that their experienced employees may view these activities as inappropriate for a leader. You need to realise that a failure to harmonize work styles, or to ensure that the work style you prefer is understood and supported by the team, can have a negative impact. As Clorox stated, "the lack of commonality in work styles doesn't result in a relationship of trust, in turn impacting the commitment of older workers to their managers."

For Traditionalists, there is a preference for working in a very linear fashion, where one task is completed at a time (e.g. you don't start another task or abandon the current one until you have finished what you started). They often perceive the way the younger generations work as disorganized and scattered. Similarly, Baby Boomers like structure, because structure means that there is a right way and a wrong way of doing something. Since they have been exposed to a very competitive workplace environment, understanding and knowing the rules of 'the game' means that Baby Boomers can figure out how to win at the game, or how to hold others accountable to playing by the rules. Baby Boomers may find the way Gen Xers and Gen Ys work as sloppy, disjointed and potentially unprofessional. When leading experienced employees, consider how to support a work style that best meets their desires for a structured work environment.

2. Communication

Across the four generations, there are distinct opinions on what style and medium of communication is appropriate. Baby Boomers and Traditionalists complain about the lack of face to face communication skills of younger employees and, in particular, the casualness Gen Ys exude with both customers and leaders. The younger generations are frustrated with the number of face to face meetings they must attend, which are too long and don't result in action-items or accountabilities being determined. Also, with the prevalence of email and web-based tools (including surveys, blogs, virtual meeting software and live chat), younger employees often feel that these tools are more efficient and productive methods of communication. Given the opposing opinions of each generation, younger employees and more experienced employees often don't understand each other's motives and behaviours, which results in a communication breakdown.

In a Traditionalist work environment (which still exists today in some organizations), communication is top-down, meaning that the opinions and suggestions of employees are rarely solicited. Experiencing this reality did not sit well with Baby Boomers, who were focused on collective action, and who fought to have their voices heard. When they entered the workplace, they wanted to make sure that there was greater openness, consensus building, and buy-in at the team level. This resulted in meetings and activities that encouraged discussion and the validation of opinions. As a result, more time was spent in face to face meetings, since the technology of conference calls and collaborative internet sharing was not available. Many Baby Boomers believe that relationships and trust can only be built through personal, direct contact. Gen Xers leverage traditional technologies, such as email and conference calls, to facilitate communication with a large group of colleagues. Gen Ys adopt interactive mediums, such as instant messaging, social networking and text messages, to communicate just-in-time.

When communicating with your more experienced employees, use a blended communication style to ensure you are not depending too heavily on technology and alienating employees who may desire more face time with you.

3. Risk Tolerance

The level of risk tolerance is very different between the generations. This is not as a result of any pre-disposition, but rather it is the result of exposure to rapid changes and disruptive technologies, like the internet. Gen X and Gen Y generally have a higher risk tolerance than their Baby Boomer and Traditionalist colleagues do. The dot-com era saw many Gen Xers take risks, and be enormously financially successful at a young age. While each generation has had its share of successful entrepreneurs (from Ford to Facebook's Zuckerberg), the perception today is that being entrepreneurial is much easier than it has ever been before. Universities teach courses in entrepreneurism, associations are designed to help young entrepreneurs succeed, and we have a culture of entrepreneurism that is celebrated in the popular media through TV shows, such as *Shark Tank* and *Dragon's Den*.

Another factor that has contributed to a higher level of risk tolerance for Gen Xers and Gen Ys, is the fact that they are the 'beta-generations'. They grew up during an era where companies, such as Microsoft, released beta-versions of software, asking user groups to help them improve it. As a result, the younger generations tend to adopt an 80/20 rule. If a project, policy, process or procedure is 80% of the way complete, it is ready for public release, and the last 20% can be fixed after going live.

Contrasting this, Baby Boomers grew up in a world that demanded perfectionism. Raised and managed by Traditionalists who were extremely detail-oriented, being perfect was a way for Baby Boomers to differentiate themselves from each other. In a highly competitive workplace, perfection was required to move up the organizational ladder. This meant that the tested-and-true approach was preferred over new, and potentially, risky ideas due to this generation's general fear of failure and imperfection.

When you face a situation where your more experienced employees need to take more risks to achieve a project goal/business target, provide the tools and support required to ensure that they are comfortable. Reinforce that taking risks (that are well calculated and planned) is desired, even if they result in some occasional negative outcomes that can be managed.

4. Respect

Perhaps one of the most talked about factors of differentiation is the notion of respect – how each generation accords it, and what the implications are if you don't demonstrate respect in a particular way. The older generations respect authority based on title, seniority and tenure. At a colleague level, longer tenure in an organization made someone a more valuable employee than a newer colleague. Therefore, a seasoned colleague deserved more respect than others. For the younger generations, time spent on the job or title holds less value than someone's competency and ability to actually get the job done. As a result of these two divergent viewpoints, the four generations behave differently toward colleagues, managers and senior leaders who hold positions of power.

Traditionalists and Baby Boomers recognize how their relationship to senior leaders may affect their ability to climb the organizational ladder or to keep their jobs during difficult economic times. Therefore, they demonstrate respect to those in more senior positions based on seniority and title. In particular, Baby Boomers are far more astute about office politics than Gen Xers or Gen Ys, since they were raised with the warning 'be careful, your colleague today could be your boss tomorrow'. The vast majority of organizations are still hierarchical, whether overtly or tacitly, thus Gen Xers and Gen Ys often ruffle feathers when they don't behave in a way that aligns with how those in power expect to be treated. Younger employees don't see title, tenure or seniority as being the key factors for earning respect. Rather, competency and skills are more important. Regardless of level, respect is given to those who are high performers.

The best way to demonstrate respect to your experienced employees is to acknowledge their years of experience in the industry /sector/department/organization and to validate their expertise level. Comment on their past successes (those achieved prior to you leading the team), and how you will work with them to achieve similar positive results.

5. Time

Misunderstandings often occur between the experienced and the younger generations about the relationship between time spent at the office vs. time spent doing 'work'. Many Baby Boomers grew up in an environment where dedication to the job was measured by the number of hours spent in the office. Clorox told us that there is a perception by experienced workers that "work is prioritized differently by younger generations. Experienced generations will sometimes put all else aside to get their work done." This value was passed down by Traditionalists, who often retired at the end of their careers with weeks of unused vacation and sick time accrued. To be successful, Baby Boomers had to model themselves after their Traditionalist colleagues and managers. Early in their careers, they learned that arriving at work 15 minutes before their managers and leaving 15 minutes later meant that they were perceived to be very hard working. They realized that having their ideas implemented, or getting promoted, took time and dedication. 'Short-term' for Baby Boomers meant 2-3 years, not 2-3 months as a Gen Xer would perceive it, or 2-3 weeks as Gen Ys would perceive it. Today, Baby Boomers demonstrate that same time commitment by sending emails at all hours of the night and during weekends, showing that they are never 'off'.

In contrast, the younger generations' motto is to work smarter, not harder. Gen Xers focus on achieving results with the maximum amount of time efficiency, so that they can leave the office or spend time on more interesting assignments. Gen Ys believe that their employment contract is fulfilled by meeting the contracted number of hours per week. They struggle with working longer hours, unless the project or task interests them or helps to build specific skills sets. For this cohort, it is a very rational business arrangement, and they do not understand why it would be expected that they give 'free labour' to their employer, unless there is an explicit return on investment for them in investing the time.

It is important to recognize that your experienced employees want to demonstrate their commitment to you by investing in long hours or modelling your work style. Be clear about your expectations on 'face-time', and when you expect them to stop their working day.

APPLY

Regardless of your generational identity, it is important that you demonstrate a leadership style that engages and motivates experienced employees. This requires you to become an effective situational leader, by focusing on the following actions:

Acknowledge personal value judgments

- Without being conscious of it, we all judge each other through our respective and diverse lenses – be it gender, culture, orientation, or generational identity. Once you have identified what value judgements you hold, you must then have a conversation with your employees about what is important to you, and actively listen to what they value. Ask open-ended questions that allow you to seek to understand differing viewpoints, particularly as it relates to work style, communication, respect, time, and risk tolerance.

Learn from employees' expertise

- Traditionalists and Baby Boomers have had years of experience working in their roles, in your organization, and in your industry. They have both functional and tacit knowledge (regarding relationship dynamics, office politics etc.) that they can, and want to, share with you. Ask your experienced employees specific questions that are directly related to your project goals or personal development interests. You will find that you will be better prepared as a leader, and that your team members will also be more engaged.

Create greater team collaboration

- One of your key accountabilities as a leader is to ensure that all team members collaborate effectively towards common team goals. If you are leading a multigenerational team, hold special meetings where the objective is for team members to share their areas of expertise with each other. These meetings don't need to be long, nor does every team member need to share every time, but the objective is to encourage knowledge transfer between team members, and to create an environment where all levels of experience are respected and valued.

Recognize the contributions of experienced employees

- For Traditionalists and Baby Boomers, public recognition is important. When an experienced employee has done a good job, send an email and 'cc' a higher level manager (the higher, the better), or acknowledge his/her contribution at the next team meeting, and invite a higher level manager to attend. It might also be helpful to have colleagues speak to the employee's high performance. This shows the value the employee has made to the organization, as well as to the team.

Use formal feedback mechanisms

- Experienced employees tend to appreciate a more structured approach to feedback, where younger employees might desire informality. While all generations like to understand the rules of the game, Baby Boomers judge how they are doing in the game through the formal process, as opposed to the younger generations, who are inclined to self-evaluate, and then tell their managers how well they think they are performing. Ensure that, when you are giving feedback to Traditionalists or Baby Boomers, you begin and end with the wins/successes, and sandwich areas of development in the middle of the conversation. Lastly, don't make the mistake of thinking that experienced employees do not want to continue to learn and grow, simply because of their age. Make sure that you ask experienced employees about their development desires.

Provide learning support

- Experienced employees don't necessarily resist change, but they are inclined to be more cautious of change. Change in their careers has not always been positive, as it has often lead to the abandonment of projects that they were leading, restructuring of their positions, or even lay-offs. When announcing changes to the team, make sure that you explain how experienced employees' skill sets will remain valuable. Also, make sure to explain what kind of formal and informal training will be provided to support employees in successfully implementing a change initiative.

Show compassion for life-events

- Any employee can have a catastrophic life event but, given an aging population, it is more likely that your experienced employees will deal with catastrophic life issues, such as illness or the death of a loved one. It is important that you create a work environment that supports a work-life balance, especially for your Baby Boomer employees who may be sandwiched between the stresses associated with raising children and caring for aging parents. Since many Baby Boomers believe that their time spent at work is a marker of their value, it's important that you support employees by letting them know that you value their personal and professional well-being. At Clorox, they make a conscious effort to encourage team members to experiment with the flexibility that younger workers take for granted. For example, when a Baby Boomer was encouraged to work from home, she realized that working remotely did not equate to slacking, and her perspective of flexibility changed.

UPGRADE

While this entire chapter has provided a generational perspective to leading and managing, it is important to highlight some fundamental underlying considerations. Ageism works both ways. The older generations have their perceptions of younger employees and colleagues that are often not positive. However, the younger generations need to recognize that they also make judgments about older employees and colleagues. Often, discrimination is directed at the older worker. For example, when an older employee is hired into an entry-level position, his/her younger peers may assume that s/he is not as competent.

> Research indicates that supervisors rate older subordinates lower, other things being equal, perhaps because of the sense that such subordinates would have been promoted already if they were really good workers. Evidence also suggests that managers tend to explain problems with performance differently for older workers: they are more likely to blame poor performance in older workers on ability or character issues and are less likely to recommend training as a solution than they would for equivalent younger workers.[3]

It is also important to acknowledge the perceptions that Baby Boomers have of younger employees. Baby Boomers have grown up in a world in which they were taught to respect elders, so they have that expectation even of younger leaders, as it relates to their status.[4] Clorox pointed out one of the major generational judgments: Younger managers don't have or sometimes appreciate the wisdom that experienced workers bring to the position (i.e. tenure, experiences). Younger managers believe that the knowledge and expertise that experienced generations possess can be replaced by searching the internet versus talking to experienced workers. In turn, experienced employees seem to retreat into themselves, which unfortunately impacts performance.

Additionally, Baby Boomers, who are by nature highly competitive, believe that experience trumps education. Thus, younger leaders who may have gone to school longer and who have higher academic credentials cannot rely on their education alone for respect or proof of their value to the team. Baby Boomers believe that achievement should only come after the payment of dues, which consist of working long hours and sacrificing pleasure for work. They are more individualistic and want to be recognized for their specific contributions.[5] Many Boomers and Traditionalists who report to younger leaders feel that those younger leaders have not sufficiently sacrificed to earn that position. These emotional and rational hurdles are the ones that younger leaders must be able to overcome, in order to engage Baby Boomers and Traditionalists.

EXECUTE

Use this evaluation tool to assist you in leading and managing experienced employees. Answer each question, and review semi-annually to ensure that you are remaining aware of your own leadership style and practices.

1. Describe your expectations regarding the following concepts (what's important/not important):

   - Work style
   - Communication
   - Risk tolerance
   - Respect
   - Time

2. Is your leadership most aligned to your age cohort (Gen X or Gen Y) or do you demonstrate a style that is similar to more experienced leaders in your organization?

3. What is the generational make-up of your team? Do most employees demonstrate the values, behaviours and expectations of the experienced generations or the younger generations?

4. What do you feel you currently do well in leading your team?

    - Acknowledge personal value judgments
    - Learn from employees' expertise
    - Create greater team collaboration
    - Recognize the contributions of experienced employees
    - Use formal feedback mechanisms
    - Provide learning support
    - Show compassion for life-events

5. What actions can you adopt or improve, based on your understanding of the experienced generations' needs and expectations?

    - Acknowledge personal value judgments
    - Learn from employees' expertise
    - Create greater team collaboration
    - Recognize the contributions of experienced employees
    - Use formal feedback mechanisms
    - Provide learning support
    - Show compassion for life events

6. What barriers have you faced in leading more experienced employees? How can you overcome these barriers?

8 LEADING AND MANAGING CHANGE

Leading and Managing Change

LEARN

Change management is a combination of two concepts – the process of change and the act of management. *Change* is defined as 'becoming different; making a shift; and undergoing a transformation or transition.' *Management* means 'directing with a degree of skill; conducting or supervising something.' Thus, change management requires both an understanding of the elements of change, and an understanding about how to lead others successfully through change. In a business context, it is about managing change so that you can realize business results. To understand your role in managing change, it is important to be clear on what change management is and is not.

Change Management is:	Change Management is not:
▪ The processes, tools and techniques for managing the people-side of change	▪ A stand-alone process for designing solutions
▪ A method for reducing and managing resistance to the change process	▪ A process improvement method
▪ A key component for any organizational performance improvement process to succeed	▪ A separate technique for improving organizational performance

While you may not be responsible for initiating or leading a major change initiative, as a leader you will be required to implement changes and, most importantly, to lead your teams through the change process.

Change management is a complex process involving several different levels:

Types of Change

Stages of Change

Obstacles to Change

Reactions to Change

10 Steps

Types of Change

At a very macro level, there are essentially only two types of change you will need to manage – organizational change and individual change. *Organizational change* involves changes the business undertakes to improve, which could include new processes, technology, organizational structure, products/services, or business models.

Organizational changes can be either:

Developmental

- Improving on something that already exists, such as a technical solution to increase efficiency

Transitional

- Something new, with known end results, that fits within the current cultural and behavioural approach, such as a new performance-based pay structure

Transformative

- Something entirely new, with unknown results, requiring cultural and behavioural changes, such as a merger / acquisition or disinvestment of a business unit[1]

Regardless of the type of organizational change that is being implemented, as a leader, you need to be able to identify how to assist your employees through the change while maintaining engagement and productivity.

Individual change involves the process that each employee undergoes during his/her own personal transition through change. This is the people side of change. It is the most difficult element of the change management process, and is, often, most poorly managed by leaders. Successful organizational change is completely dependent on effective individual change.

> "*Implementing organizational change initiatives invariably involves people changing themselves. The change you want to make cannot happen until people decide to change...change is situational...transition is the psychological process people go through to come to terms with the new situation. Unless transition takes place, the planned change will simply not work.*"[2]

Stages of Individual Change for Employees

Regardless of the type of organizational change you are leading, the research indicates that there are three stages employees must go through to ensure change is solidified.

Stage 1 – Undoing

Before change can occur, employees need to let go of their old way of doing things or their old identity. This can create a strong sense of loss from attachments they have had and to routines they have followed. Whether real or perceived, feelings of loss around what was certain and stable exist, even in cases when change is for the better. At this stage, it is important that there be a strong motivation for change by employees, coupled with clear communication by the leader as to what the vision for the future will look like.

Stage 2 – Learning

In stage two, employees must learn new concepts or new ways of doing things. This will occur through trial-and-error learning. It typically causes a temporary state of disorientation as it is an 'in-between' time, when the comforts of the old are gone, but the new reality hasn't fully formed yet. At this stage, it is important that there are role models to demonstrate the new behaviours, attitudes, and tasks.

Stage 3 – Locking In

The final stage is locking in and internalizing the new concepts /behaviours/actions, so that change can be solidified. At this point, employees are able to make a new beginning by adopting a new way of doing things or creating a new identity. It is important that employees can attach a sense of purpose to what they now do, so that the change can be successful. At this stage, people let go of the past and incorporate the new reality into their self-concept.[3]

One of the reasons why change initiatives fail is that leaders often don't plan for what is required to lead their teams through the undoing, learning and locking in. They often fail to identify the behaviours that must be demonstrated and the milestones that must be reached before employees are ready to fully adopt the change. The transition through the three stages must occur before change management can be fully realized. Your role is to identify your employees' stage and to support them in moving through the process. If employees remain stuck in the undoing stage, new learning will not occur. If they stagnate at the learning stage, execution won't fully take place. All employees must reach the locking in stage to ensure that the change takes root.

Identifying Obstacles to Change

Unfortunately, at some point in the process, you will likely encounter obstacles to your change initiative. There are several factors that can negatively affect your ability to implement change, but none are as significant as a lack of senior leadership support. This is the most significant barrier to your success, second only to unrealistic top management expectations.

Your success in guiding employees through change depends on your ability to maintain on-going support from key stakeholders and securing the resources required to execute your plans to help employees transition. If you encounter resistance to change from other leaders, you may need to actively engage more senior people to help gain their buy-in. Our client, Chevron, recommends that "upper management should take a closer look at, and a more aggressive approach in, engaging any reluctant leader early on in shaping the change management process."

Other common problems that derail change initiatives include changes that are too complex and shifting priorities. Finally, at an individual employee level, you will likely experience obstacles that will impact your success, such as:

- Employees who are distracted by the change, thus impacting their performance levels
- High performing employees who leave the organization
- Increased absenteeism
- Cynicism about the change
- Information overload
- Fear of the unknown, resulting in resistance to the change

To be successful, you must be aware of the obstacles that can occur, prepare for how to overcome them, and proactively take action to minimize their impact.

Reactions to Change

The reality is that approximately 70% of all change initiatives fail.[4] This is not encouraging news for leaders, who are often directed by senior levels to execute a change initiative and to 'make it happen'. To be successful, you need to understand the process employees undergo when faced with a substantial change, so that you can manage *reactions* to change.

It should be assumed that employees will initially resist significant changes and that some will never support the change. Your role as a leader is to overcome this barrier by supporting employees (with guidance, tools and training) during change in order to help them effectively manage the transition. To do so, you need to be able to put yourself in your employees' shoes. Fundamentally, leaders and employees often perceive change initiatives very differently. Leaders tend to see change as a way to improve the business, while employees often see change as disruptive, intrusive, and possibly frightening.

This gap in perception exists because, in most cases, leaders are the initiators of change (those who design and implement the change) and employees are the bearers of change (those who are impacted by the change, but not involved in the design). Often, the bearers of change have not been engaged in discussions involving the decision to implement a change and, therefore, do not feel real ownership over the process or outcome. "Most change efforts involve people only after all the big decisions are made, ignoring the tendency for people to support that which they have a hand in creating and to resist other change."[5]

Generally, we all respond to change by going through four phases, which are similar to the grieving process. They are:

1. Shock
2. Defensive retreat
3. Acknowledgement
4. Acceptance and adaptation[6]

Your role as a leader is to evaluate and acknowledge where employees are in relation to these four phases, and to help them move through to acceptance. In interviewing Chevron, we learned that their approach to helping employees move through the change process includes: training on the benefits of the change; involving employees during the planning stages; discussing potential challenges to adoption; and identifying resources that can be provided to assist. Resistance to change is the norm, not the exception. However, leaders often label employees who don't immediately and wholeheartedly embrace change as 'difficult'.

> *Executives commonly believe that if they can execute a change programme the 'right' way, people will be on board with the changes. That is not necessarily true. Resistance is a natural part of the change process. With every change, some assumption or habitual way of doing things is broken and every such break is a loss. Thus employees resist change because they are human, not because they are disloyal or incompetent. Unless executives understand that dynamic, they are likely to take actions that only make matters worse – using threats, power plays or communications that cast the resistors as unintelligent or not 'team players'[7]*

Our client Scotiabank has found that employees are often re-sistant to change, if you try to move them too quickly through the process. They will ask 'why?' or 'what's the point?' The organization engages employees in the change process by communicating early on the overall strategy and objectives. They also highlight how the objectives are supported through the individual changes that employees will be making (including what they do day-to-day). It is the leader's role to provide a strong linkage to overall objectives, to provide a clear rationale for why the change is occurring, and to communicate frequent updates. "When you do a good job of communicating and clarifying, the change no longer strikes employees as an adaptive challenge, but rather their response is 'of course we should be doing that!"(Scotiabank).

APPLY

Despite the number of obstacles to change, the emotional reactions employees can have to change, and the tendency to initially resist change, there are a number of factors that can set you up for success:

Engage

- Gain senior leadership support by creating a sense of urgency; 75% of leaders need to be convinced that 'business as usual' is unacceptable[8]
- Keep leaders involved throughout the length of the change initiative
- Identify leaders who will act as role models

Communicate

- Identify a clear, shared vision for change
- Deliver targeted, on-going communication to employees throughout the initiative
- Clarify roles, commitments and accountabilities of all employees
- Involve senior leaders through formal communication messages delivered by them

Manage

- Avoid scope drift – contain the change to the business unit/team/individuals that need to change
- Assume responsibility and ownership for the implement-tation of the plan, or the portion of the plan that is within your scope. Don't rely on human resources or senior leaders to execute your plan
- Conduct frequent status reviews throughout the life of the project
- Anchor the change into your organizational, department, or team culture

Support

- Listen without judgement
- Keep as many other things as possible intact and consistent
- Create a sense of urgency around the need for change
- Describe the future rationally and in a business context
- Assume responsibility and accountability for leading the change
- Personalize the benefits of change
- Solicit opinions and ideas
- Openly and honestly address employees' concerns and anxieties
- Transition the conversation from emotions to productive actions employees can take to embrace the change
- Lead by example by 'walking the talk'
- Empower employees to implement changes by delegating responsibility

In order to effectively implement a change you will need to: identify which type of change it is (developmental, transitional, or transformative); predict which barriers might arise for you; plan how to support employees in their reactions to the change; and overcome resistance.

UPGRADE

The acceptance of change and the willingness to embrace it is largely dependent on the change experiences employees have had in the past. Each generation holds a different view of change based on their shared experiences. No one generation is more or less likely to resist change; there will be resisters to change from all four generations. As noted previously, change can trigger emotional reactions, where a deep sense of loss is felt most profoundly by those who are accustomed to or desire stability. Traditionalists enjoy their lives of stable, long-term employment with one organization, life-time marriage, and living in the same community or home for decades. Given their desire for stability, their tendency is to want to minimize change in their professional lives. Many Traditionalists work for the same employer for their entire careers, perhaps in the same department or even in the same role for years.

In a Traditionalist's world, change only happened when there was a good reason for it. It was not undertaken lightly and, if things were working (think organizational practices/processes), they remained the same. This cohort has strong beliefs that "if it ain't broke, don't fix it". This attitude has led many organizations and leaders to maintain the status quo, because "that's the way we have always done it." Traditionalists resist changes that are perceived to be lacking substantial benefit. For change to be accepted, it must be linked to how it will benefit the organization at a macro and strategic level, with a long-term view in mind. A change must fix an existing problem. If a change is deemed by Traditionalist employees to be simply popular or political in nature, they will be unlikely to support the change.

Baby Boomers tend to be cautious of change. Their reluctance isn't a result of not wanting to seek improvements, but a result of the fact that many Baby Boomers lost their jobs during the recessions of the '80s and '90s, which made them shy of broad organizational changes. Baby Boomers have experienced a lot of changes in their careers and, with every change in senior leadership, organizational changes have followed. They have had to endure 'flavour of the month' leadership changes, as well as shifts back and forth in strategy (such as decentralization to centralizations, or horizontal markets to vertical ones). This see-saw of change has contributed to this generation feeling 'change fatigue' which translates into a lack of enthusiasm for new changes, and can be misinterpreted by leaders as resistance. In principle, Baby Boomer employees may not resist the change. They may simply be less excited about it than younger generations, if they believe the change will be short lived.

This generation is very politically savvy, and therefore will be careful to only support changes they believe will also be supported by more senior leaders, or changes that will raise their profile in the organization. Baby Boomers approach change initiatives with a critical view, by 'poking holes' in the project before committing to it. As rebellious as this cohort was before entering the work world, Baby Boomers need to understand how a change benefits their team/department, and how it contributes to their professional status before jumping on board. A Baby Boomer employee may feel a sense of loss if asked to take on a lesser part in the change. Their concern is that it that might affect their profile in the organization, even if the change is an enhancement in other ways, such as increased pay or deeper skill sets.

Generation X is skeptical of leaders' motivations and intentions when implementing change. They want to know the benefits of the change, most notably to them, and what they will gain by adopting a new approach. Gen Xers view change as an opportunity to improve, be it their position, skill sets or relationships with colleagues and leaders. They must understand and accept what's in it for them, before supporting the initiative. But, once that is achieved, they will act as great champions for change. Since this generation witnessed corporate downsizing, the dot-com bubble burst, and the scandals in the financial sectors, they expect change to happen and, often, aren't surprised with radical shifts at an organizational or team level. Resistance occurs if they believe the change will hinder their ability to achieve results. Since this generation is focused on gaining marketable skills and results for their resume, they want to focus on the quantifiable results the change will achieve. This cohort also expects to be rewarded for implementing the change quickly and adopting the new way of doing business. If involved in the planning process, Gen Xers will focus on setting targets for how performance increases as a result of the change.

Gen Ys have grown up in a world where change is constant, where technology changes every 3 – 6 months. Gen Ys don't long for the past, but rather are constantly seeking the newest, latest improvement. Software is constantly being updated, hardware is being enhanced, and change is about making things faster, better, cooler. Therefore, change equals an improvement. This has translated into a culture where Gen Y employees expect organizational changes to occur quickly and frequently. This cohort can become quite frustrated with organizations and teams where there is a slower pace of change, or a reluctance to change at all. In addition to the speed of change, this generation also desires real change, not simply lip service. For years Gen Ys have expressed to us their frustration with leaders who say they want change, but don't act quickly, don't implement significant changes, or don't hold all employees responsible for adopting the change. It is important to focus on the short-term successes of a change initiative in order to demonstrate to this cohort that progress is being made. Unlike older generations, who tend to want to plan every detail of a change initiative, Gen Ys are comfortable with implementing a change, even if it isn't entirely perfect. In a world where you can upgrade your software or download a new version, there is no need to wait until every detail is perfect. Instead, you make adjustments as needed, in real time. This approach is drastically different than many organizational cultures and can cause friction between team members involved in implementing a change. This cohort is eager to add value and to express their opinions, so involving them in identifying and planning for potential changes is particularly important in getting this generation on side. Resistance to change happens if the initiative is entirely driven top-down, or if there is a sense that the change is too minor and insignificant to make an impact.

EXECUTE

To assist in implementing a change initiative, this 10-step process document provides you with a list of what to do, and how to do it, to ensure you can effectively manage both the operational and people side of the change process.

Step	Actions
1. Initiate	▪ Analyze organization's ability and willingness to change ▪ Evaluate organization's track record for past change initiatives ▪ Formalize concept of change (type and complexity) ▪ Develop scenarios showcasing what could happen if change isn't implemented ▪ Gain senior leadership commitment ▪ Identify a clear, shared vision for change
2. Plan	▪ Determine the values that are central to the change ▪ Design a customized solution that aligns with organizational/team culture ▪ Engage external advisors as needed ▪ Document the plan ▪ Collect baseline data ▪ Review plan with all stakeholders ▪ Gain senior leadership sign-off

Step	Actions
3. Build	▪ Build an experienced team – select employees who will be affected by the change and involved in the execution ▪ Line up political sponsors ▪ Leverage internal experts to build a custom solution ▪ Clarify roles, commitments and accountabilities of all team members
4. Communicate (ongoing)	▪ Build a communication strategy – identify multiple touch points, using multiple mediums ▪ Communicate your change vision to all employees in simple and clear language ▪ Leverage technology to communicate broadly (website, webinars, live chat etc.) ▪ Create a feedback loop to collect employee feelings/opinions ▪ Listen actively
5. Remove Obstacles (on-going)	▪ Identify barriers and their root causes ▪ Negotiate to achieve a win-win outcome ▪ Seek input from employees on the obstacles they are facing

Step	Actions
6. Execute	▪ Implement your plan – take action ▪ Conduct training for employees as required ▪ Create an environment that supports the change ▪ Leverage change agents and supporters ▪ Lead by example
7. Evaluate	▪ Track and monitor progress against the plan ▪ List obstacles encountered ▪ Capture lessons learned ▪ Adjust the plan as required and communicate to all
8. Celebrate Successes	▪ Celebrate small successes on a frequent basis ▪ Reward employees/teams who achieve goals
9. Anchor Change	▪ Embed the change into the culture of 'how things are done' ▪ Reinforce behaviours/actions that support the change ▪ Set goals to continue building on the momentum achieved
10. Calculate ROI	▪ Collect results and compare to baseline data ▪ Gather qualitative feedback on the success or failure of the project

9 LEVERAGING SOCIAL MEDIA

Leveraging Social Media

Social media has become part of our daily lives for communicating and building relationships. For several years, organizations and leaders have been aware that employees are using these tools in their personal lives, but they have been reluctant to allow and incorporate them into the business environment. Today, even the most traditionalist environments have adopted some form of social media. It's futile to resist the adoption of these technologies, just as it was futile in the past to place barriers on personal computers and e-mail.

There are countless definitions of 'social media', but fundamentally they are "technologies designed to facilitate social interactions, communication, and, sometimes, publishing."[1] These technologies are generally internet-based and are used to support 'many-to-many' conversations, versus traditional 'one-to-many' media broadcasts.

There are dozens of social media tools available to users, including most notably:

Medium Type	Example	Medium Type	Example
Social networks	Facebook	Pictures	Flickr
Blogs	Ask	Virtual worlds	Second Life
Workspaces	SharePoint	Live chatting	Skype
Networks	LinkedIn	Podcasts	iTunes
Videos	YouTube	Image sharing	Instagram
Wikis	Wikipedia	Life streams	eHarmony

These tools are categorized as Web 2.0 technologies, because of their ability to engage users. "Typical websites are controlled by one person or organization, with the purpose of simply pushing out information; social media sites, on the other hand, invite users to actually respond. In fact, the vast majority of content on social networking sites (or social media) comes from the public itself. Web users have the most control over what content goes on the site, with free reign to log on and post comments, links, photos, videos or responses to other users' posts."[2]

Thus, social media are:

- Web-based and mobile technologies used to turn communication into interactive dialogue
- Media designed to be disseminated through social interaction, created using highly accessible and scalable publishing techniques
- Media that is created to be shared freely
- Works of user-created video, audio, text or multimedia that are published and shared in a social environment
- The use of technology combined with social interaction to create or co-create value

The use of social media is now completely widespread. Nearly half (48%) of all Americans have social networking profiles, which has doubled since 2008[3] and 2 billion YouTube videos are viewed each day.[4] Research conducted by us in 2009 revealed that 66% of all Canadians accessed social media at work, with the highest usage being from Gen Ys (81%).[5] Today, that usage has increased, with employees estimating that they spend four hours a day managing their electronic 'inboxes'. In addition, social networking sites, such as Facebook, have now blurred the lines between business and personal use and encourage an intermingling of the two worlds. Often, it's no longer a clear cut case of what is and isn't a 'business related activity'.

Benefits

There are numerous benefits to organizations, leaders and employees of integrating social media within current work practices. In fact, those teams who are embracing social media are reaping the rewards of:

- Increased productivity and performance
- Stronger internal relationships
- Increased communication - inspiring open and honest dialogue
- Improved knowledge management - transferring, collecting, sharing
- Greater creativity through exposure to differing thoughts / perspectives
- Increased employee engagement and morale
- Enhanced connection with customers/clients through real-time conversations
- Improved transparency
- Targeted marketing of products and services
- Faster problem solving and testing of ideas, thus reducing planning cycles
- Reduced costs for travel

Research has shown that 52% of organizations using Web 2.0 technologies have achieved best-in-class performance, have increased engagement by 18%, and have saved significant dollars. Our client, Cisco, attributes millions of dollars in savings to their use of wikis.[6] In addition to these benefits, your organization's long-term capabilities will be strengthened, which is a major driver in attracting and retaining top employees. Not only can social media enhance the productivity and performance of your team, but it can also improve your ability to connect with candidates and promote your organizational values, strategies and branding to your target audience. Ultimately, social media represents a change in how we communicate, interact, work, and create. It is challenging us to think differently, and for you to lead your team differently, by leveraging the tools you have available to achieve your business goals and engage employees in the right way, at the right time.

Barriers

Despite the benefits gained by using social media, many organizations and leaders struggle conceptually with adopting technology that shifts power from the top of the organization and spreads it more evenly throughout the organization. "Within organizations, social media demonstrates the new reality – that employees are co-creators of organizational success rather than servants of the company who simply salute and take orders."[7] Fundamentally, social media is impacting the ability of leaders to adhere to a strictly top-down management style. The focus shifts from one person knowing and possessing all the information, to a free flow of knowledge, information and innovation which resides within differing layers of every organization through 'managed anarchy'.[8] The open and collaborative environment created by using any Web 2.0 technology can make senior leaders very uncomfortable, since it bucks against the formal, rigid structures. It challenges core assumptions about how work should be done.

Social networks are predicated on two-way communication, which empowers employees to voice their opinions and thoughts and allows them to be heard in a meaningful way. In this new Social Age, each person's opinion carries equal weight, everyone's credibility is enhanced, and all contributions are important. This is particularly relevant in crowd sourcing, where decision making is achieved through the opinions of the collective group.[9] The first response senior leaders may take is to contain, control or stop the use of these collaborative networks, rather than to leverage them.

From a purely business perspective, often the resistance to social media is due to concerns about: the loss of productivity; the IT resources required for administration and high bandwidth issues; the ability to control the corporate brand and reputation; and, the legal issues arising from the use of these technologies. From an individual perspective, some leaders are reluctant to adopt social media, since they fear they won't have time to incorporate it into their already busy workdays. At Cisco, they view this as a non-issue as it's a misconception to believe that one needs to stop what they are doing to make a concerted effort to use social media. Instead, they recommend that people view web 2.0 tools as just another resource, which can be leveraged the same way as any other reference or resource.

Approaches to Social Media Use

Social media promotes conversations and relationships and puts people at the centre. It is more a 'state of mind' than a technology, and requires that, as a leader, you examine ways to leverage these technologies to improve transparency, collaboration, productivity, and knowledge transfer. To do so, you must implement a social media strategy that is based on trust and taps into employees' innovation, creativity and enthusiasm.

There are three approaches that organizations take in addressing social media use:

1. Ban access to social networking sites
2. Set limits and restrictions on use
3. Allow unmonitored access[10]

Fundamentally, your social media policy will be based on the degree to which your organization and leaders trust employees. However, the ability to ban or restrict access will become increasingly difficult. Tools, such as Microsoft Outlook, now have components that integrate Facebook, LinkedIn, My Space, and Windows Live into their software, which reflects how social media is a becoming a normal tool of office communication.[11] Organizations that choose to severely restrict access to social media do so out of a fear that their brand will be negatively impacted by inappropriate posts that are deemed insensitive, racist, vulgar, or that leak confidential information. Organizations that provide guidelines and training on how to properly use social media do so with a focus on increasing brand awareness through employee empowerment and trust.

Depending on your scope of influence, you may or may not be able to directly impact your organization's formal social media policy. However, you can look for ways that your team can leverage Web 2.0 tools in order to improve your ability to work collaboratively with employees and demonstrate that you trust their judgement. Since a culture of trust is essential for high levels of employee engagement, performance and retention, "restricting access to social media (and other) websites might actually cost you money due to 'higher than it might be' staff turnover rates."[12]

Studies have shown that having looser control on how social media is used and accessed at work has resulted in 40-65% of activity posted during the work day to be professional in nature, focusing on either requesting or sharing information with colleagues.[13] At IBM, employees are encouraged to talk to each other and the public, without regulation or monitoring. Forums are self-regulated. The results are highly interactive exchanges of ideas, conversations and promotion of innovative projects through IBM's own SocialBlue site, which acts like Facebook, and BlueTwit which mimics Twitter.[14] Similarly, Cisco allows unmonitored use, and provides guidelines and a business conduct policy to employees that emphasises the same principles that would be applied to any public communication – do not act as a representative of the company or reveal any intellectual property.

If you don't trust your team to communicate through social media, and to use good judgement, you likely have a hiring problem, not a social media problem. Employees that abuse the system were probably bad hires. Those that you can trust will become ambassadors for your brand, and will demonstrate the positive effects of a less rigid policy.

APPLY

Before you can properly leverage social media, you need to establish an appropriate policy. It is important to create a policy that is unique and that addresses how your team collaborates with internal and external stakeholders. The first step is to understand to what extent employees value social media and how they are currently using it. Secondly, you need to identify if there are employees who are 'cutting edge', who can help co-create the policy, and who can provide guidance to other team members on how to use the tool effectively. Finally, examine all of the ways that social media can be used – from recruiting, to training, to team meetings, to client interactions. Once you have completed these three steps, you can draft a policy that will meet the needs of employees and customers. At Scotiabank, they have created an internal social media vehicle called "Scotiabank Live" which acts as a Facebook type tool for the organization. Employees can blog, post and comment on topics of interest to them. The application is still evolving to meet the needs of leaders and employees, with recent updates, such as tools for managers and learning communities.

Many leaders wonder how they can use social media within their teams to simply improve engagement and productivity. However, you can also improve team collaboration and communication in general by:

- Using instant messaging instead of email to improve real time collaboration and rapid problem solving
- Creating a private LinkedIn group to stimulate brainstorming and pooling of information and ideas
- Leveraging your company Facebook page to connect with customers

- Having employees blog about their projects to capture and store knowledge
- Using wikis to allow employees to contribute to a body of knowledge
- Incorporating dedicated project management tools (i.e. BaseCamp) to increase collaboration with customers and team members
- Creating an internal social networking site (i.e. IBM's SocialBlue) to help employees stay connected and share information on a more personal level
- Using Skype, Live Meeting, Halo, etc. as a way of chatting live with employees that are across regions, time zones and continents

In order to ensure social media use is leveraged appropriately and effectively, you should lead by example. Take the time to familiarize yourself with various tools and identify how you can incorporate them into your existing work structure.

Encourage appropriate use of all social media by:

- Training employees on your policy and ensuring full understanding
- Trusting employees to do the right thing
- Encouraging timely responses to issues/posts
- Encouraging employees to Tweet about team members to boost morale and positive comments about the organization
- Mining social media sites to learn about customers and competitors

While all employees, at all levels, will benefit from the widespread use of social media, it is particularly important to use with virtual employees / teams as a way to increase feelings of connection with the larger team.

UPGRADE

It is no surprise that Gen Ys are the most prolific users of social media, with 78% of this cohort engaging in online activities. However, the reality is that all generations are using social media in some capacity, be it reading and contributing to blogs, watching and uploading videos on YouTube, or staying connected with friends and colleagues through Facebook or LinkedIn. In fact, more than 60% of people those over 55 years old use social media on a regular basis.[15]

Traditionalists are joining social networking sites to stay connected with their grandchildren, with an emphasis on strengthening relationships. It would be highly unlikely that a Traditionalist would post any negative comments about their employer online. This generation places an emphasis on following the rules, and therefore, will strictly adhere to your social media policy. You may need to support this cohort in learning how to use the new technology, but, once they are comfortable, they will engage in activities that keep them connected to you as a leader and to their colleagues.

Baby Boomers have significantly increased their usage of social media in the past year, up by 79%.[16] This generation is drawn to business-enhancing activities, such as podcasts for work related learning.[17] While this cohort is quick to adopt new hardware, they may be slower to use social media software to replace existing methods of communication and collaboration. Nearly half (45%) of

Baby Boomers believe that meetings are extremely necessary to decide on a course of action.[18] This desire for face-to-face communication can cause conflicts with Gen Xers and Gen Ys, who are more inclined to rely on other methods to connect. In addition, many Baby Boomer leaders feel that employees who use social media during the work day are wasting time and are not focussing on achieving business results. This attitude can create a divide between those who believe social media can be leveraged to enhance business activities, versus those who believe it's a distraction. There can be a negative perception by colleagues of those employees who are heavy users of social media, particularly if their work is suffering. In that respect, it has less to do with the technology and more to do with poor performance overall.

Gen Xers are actually the heaviest users of social media for business purposes[19], with a focus on how to better connect with colleagues and clients in order to achieve results. This cohort is quick to adopt tools that improve their ability to get things done and enhance just-in-time problem solving and decision making. Given this cohort's desire for a work-life balance, Gen Xers leverage technology to ensure they can meet personal and professional commitments within a flexible work day. Gen Xers are open to leveraging social media, if it has a direct benefit to them. Blogging about your organization, for the sake of promoting your brand, will be less appealing to Gen Xers than their ability to Tweet about their accomplishments and skills to boost their career. The use of hash tags (# symbol plus a string of text, used to mark keywords or topics in a Tweet) can help Gen X employees draw attention to their accomplishments, thus allowing leaders to see all of their achievements by clicking on that word.[20]

Gen Ys, who have grown up in the Social Age, are accustomed to using technology to communicate and connect. While the older generations might feel that technology acts as a barrier to communication, Gen Ys view it as an essential element to staying connected. In fact, this generation often requires guidance on when and how to conduct effective face to face conversations. Skills, such as business communication, project planning and leadership, can initially be lacking in this cohort due to a lack of exposure to formal, business communication methods. In contrast to the 45% of Baby Boomers who feel that meetings are extremely necessary, only 29% of Gen Ys feel the same way. The vast majority feel meetings are ineffective, especially when social media tools can be used instead.[21] Forty percent of this cohort expects to have access to social media at work[22], which supports their desire for a fluid work environment. To Gen Y, everything is fluid, so they may not understand workplace boundaries. They find an organization's attempts to block social networking sites as laughable (since most of them can access it on their hand-held devices anyway). They are least likely to be concerned that social media tools will cause security/privacy issues at work. They desire much looser restrictions on the use of social media, compared to Baby Boomers. Over three-quarters of Gen Ys believe that the use of social media at work is either somewhat or extremely useful, while only 1% consider it extremely wasteful.[23]

The research has shown that none of the generations believe organizations are leveraging social media enough[24], with Gen Ys the least satisfied. From a generational perspective, information and knowledge is perceived very differently. Once upon a time, information equalled power, and it was controlled and owned by the most senior people in an organization, and it was only distributed to others on a need-to-know basis. In the Social Age, younger (and less senior) employees desire equal access to information. From their perspective, it's not possessing information that makes one powerful, but rather what you do with the information that makes you powerful. Today, information is shared much more freely, either willingly or covertly. Rather than spending all of your time as a leader trying to control power through information hoarding, you should spend your time thinking about how to leverage information for increased engagement and productivity.

EXECUTE

Regardless of your organization's approach to social media, it is important that several components be included in your social media policy. Use the following tool to ensure you create a comprehensive policy, whether at an organizational or team level. Going through these steps will help you, as a leader, to be transparent about the appropriate use of social media.

Philosophy, Scope, and Goals

- What are you trying to achieve via social media and why? What's your definition of social media?

Common Sense and Good Judgment

- Employees need to understand your definitions of what common sense and good judgment entail (as well as what constitutes unacceptable behaviour). How do you suggest employees vet their responses? What's your guidance for "when in doubt", and who can they go to when they are uncertain whether or not to post something?

Honesty and Transparency

- Emphasize that your employees must always be open, honest, and truthful about information they share, and that they must be clear about identifying who they are. If they are making personal comments, they should make it clear that their communication is their own and not on behalf of your organization. A simple disclaimer example is "My name is X and I work for Y. The opinions I'm expressing here are my own."

Confidential and Proprietary Information

- It is critical that you explicitly state that disclosing confidential organizational information isn't permitted. It also helps to define what constitutes confidential or proprietary information, so that the boundaries are clear.

Competitor and Customer Information

- Remind employees of your stance on sharing information about customers, clients, and competitors. You may be comfortable sharing some information generally, but specific details, such as new client wins or the intricacies of your work with them, might not be something you want to share publicly. Delineate what's acceptable to share and what isn't. Be sure to include whether or not you're comfortable talking about the competition and in what capacity.

Consequences

- Clearly outline what actions will be taken if an employee does something that deliberately and negatively impacts the organization. What's the process if someone uses social media to break existing codes of conduct? It's good to outline various possibilities including everything from a warning to termination. This helps employees err on the side of safe choices, and leaves little room for interpretation, if you need to take action.

Handling and Escalating Inquiries

- If employees are officially representing your brand online or if it becomes known through their personal network that they work for your organization, media requests are a real possibility, as well as inquiries or challenges about your company activities. Give guidance on how to handle or direct media requests to the appropriate people internally. Provide training for those who will be expected to respond on behalf of your organization.

Participation During Work Hours

- Is it okay to Tweet or blog at the office, whether in an official capacity or not? It's important to set expectations about using social media during business hours. Keep in mind, it's difficult to say: "Yes, but ..." and then enforce exceptions to the rule. It's much clearer to say: "Yes, and we'll trust you to use good judgment."

Examples and Best Practices

- If you have examples of organizations whose social participation you endorse and admire, share them and point to them as positive examples of the behaviours you expect from employees.[25]

What's Next?
The Future of Leadership

The future of leadership relies on analyzing factors that will impact an organization's ability to be sustainable, as well as the skills that leaders will require to engage employees going forward. One key factor will be to continue to evaluate workforce demographics. Internal factors, such as retirement rates, succession planning, and the ability recruit and retain highly skilled employees, will remain essential. External factors, such as labour market conditions and aging workforce data, will influence how organizations and leaders will be able to meet organizational goals. n-gen was founded in 2003 to explore the impact that the four generations have on performance, and to create solutions for increasing engagement. Our first book, *Loyalty Unplugged: How to Get, Keep, and Grow All Four Generations (2007)*, helps senior leaders strategically build a workforce that motivates and engages all four generations (Traditionalists, Baby Boomers, Gen Xers and Gen Ys).

Increasingly, clients have been asking us for advice on how to prepare for the next generation that will follow Gen Ys, particularly those who hire teenage workers (retail, hospitality, tourism, parks & recreation, etc.). While it is too soon to be able to state definitely how this 5th generation will behave in the workplace, it is interesting to identify and speculate on the factors which are bound to shape them during their coming of age period (defined as the first 16 years of a person's life). While those born from 2001 onward are still being formed as a cohort, life-defining events, technology, education and parenting styles of today will impact this generation's values, behaviours, and expectations of tomorrow. Generational identities are shaped during the formative years, leading to perspectives of life and work. These perspectives, in turn, will impact the future of leadership — leaders will need to be prepared to incorporate yet another generation into an already complex multi-generational workforce. Future leadership will have to be able to adapt and respond increasingly to the new generation's expectations, while managing the existing generational mix within their teams.

Factors Shaping the "Fifth Generation": The Global Generation

n-gen has termed the fifth generation *the Global Generation* (aka The Globes), which represents those born after 2001. Like all previous generations, this cohort is being shaped by life-defining events, technology, school systems and parenting styles. For members of the Global Generation, the factors that shape them are no longer localised to their cities, regions or even countries. Their values, behaviours and expectations are being shaped by factors from all over the globe. In a world in which everything is interconnected (finance, technology, environment etc.), this generation will have a much more global point of view than previous generations. By 'global', we mean geographically and in the sense of having a broad, universal perspective, rather than a narrow perspective. While those on the cusp (born 3-4 years after 2001) may exhibit the traits of Gen Ys, there are several socioeconomic and historical factors that are bound to influence The Globes, differentiating them from Gen Ys.

We predict the factors shaping the Global Generation are:

Iraq and Afghanistan Wars: Many members of the United Nations, not just from the western world, are involved in fighting terrorism. The success of these efforts is hotly contested, as these missions are not as simple and clear cut as they were in World War II. For those born between 2001 and 2012, their countries may have always been at war.

North African and Middle Eastern Uprisings: With protests often being led by the younger populace in North Africa and the Middle East (many of these countries have a high percentage of citizens under the age of 30), it has demonstrated that en mass radical changes can happen, showing the power of the collective over a singular leader's power.

North American and European Democracy Protests: The 'Occupy' movements, the protests at G20 and G8 meetings, with high participation by young people, demonstrate an increasing concern over business, environmental and social ethics. The protestors are often concerned that the gap between the 'haves' and the 'have-nots' is increasing, not just in their own countries, but across the world.

Real Estate Meltdown: Many parents of the Global Generation are affected by the housing crisis in North America. Some families might have lost their homes, and/or have had to move. The stability that parents try to provide their children is being tested.

Global Financial Crisis: Led by a collapse on Wall Street in 2008, with reverberations throughout the entire global banking system, the recession which followed has caused many parents and relatives of The Globes to lose their jobs. While the impact varied in degrees of severity depending on the country, many families raising The Globes have been financially impacted, with many parents left unemployed or underemployed.

Mobile Technology, Social Networks and the Internet: While Gen Ys were born with computers and laptops in their homes, The Globes have been born with mobile technology at their fingertips. From infancy onward, this cohort has access to tablets and other hand-held devices. The Globes will see building friendships through social networks as the norm. They won't question whether or not to join a social network, they will simply decide upon which sites they want to set up their profiles. "They're growing up with expectations of always being present in a social way – always being available to peers wherever you are."[1] Also, this generation will be producers, and not just consumers, of information on the internet. Because of mobile technology, they can produce information just-in-time and distribute it widely, almost instantly. They are likely to become very accustomed to anonymous criticism (e.g. user comments on blogs and YouTube for example). For this generation everything is customizable, which causes frustration when they cannot control what and where they consume. They will expect innovation and portability out of everything in life.[2]

Parenting Style: The parents of the Global Generation are predominately Gen Xers (with some older Gen Ys and younger Baby Boomers also falling into this category). Gen Xers are illustrating over-protective tendencies with their children, which in part is a continuation of the Baby Boomer style of parenting. Parents of The Globes often continue to mirror the 'helicopter' parenting style of Baby Boomers (in which they hover over their children), but the overprotection is also demonstrated by increasing strictness and control over their children's lives. The latter is in opposition to the Baby Boomer style which was more free-spirited and over-indulgent. For Gen X parents, while they will listen to their children's opinions, not everything is open for negotiation. Often, the answer is 'no', with no room for compromise. Many Gen Xers have traces of a more traditionalist parenting style, in that they worry about raising children who are too materialistic, are not well-mannered, and are not prepared for the 'real world'. Given the recession and the fact that many Gen Xers have not accumulated the same levels of financial success Baby Boomers did at their age, they are raising their children with a greater sense of fiscal responsibility. Gen Xers have a fierce sense of independence, including financial independence — they are consumers, but they also monitor spending to ensure that they can protect their families.

Education System: Currently, the school system is based on a pedagogy of raising the self-esteem of students. The curriculum, policies and practices are all designed to ensure that every child is successful, and is confident in his or her abilities. However, there is starting to be discussion among educators about whether or not some of these practices are truly in the best interest of students. It may be the case that the Global Generation experiences a shift within the school system where a failing grade will once again be given for poor work, where being late (either in attendance or in meeting assignment deadlines) will have stricter consequences, or where failing a course or an entire school year will be possible. If the educational philosophies shift, then there will be a change in expectations by The Globes as to what is acceptable behaviour as it relates to responsibilities at school and work. Currently, given The Globes' rapid consumption of content, many teachers are assigning shorter books and articles, giving more condensed assignments and are incorporating more media into the classroom. Although teachers say that students are able to find answers and do research really well, there is a concern about their ability to focus on writing clearly, and to write extensive narratives. The Globes are comfortable with dichotomies and simplified explanations, but struggle with complex topics that require a deeper analysis.[3]

Based on these seven factors, we believe that the Global Generation will bring the following characteristics to the workplace:

Fiscal conservatism

- Not having grown up with the abundance that Gen Ys received from their Baby Boomer parents, The Globes are likely to be more fiscally conservative. They will have been given less, will have been expected to work for what they have, and will enter into adulthood with higher student debts (more than previous generations). Alternatively, many members of this cohort may choose more applied education that leads directly to making money in the technical, vocational or trade functions.

Expectation of complete transparency

- This generation will place less value on privacy, believing that everything should be an open book. "If you thought Gen Y was lax on privacy, the Global Generation will blow your mind."[4]

Realism

- Given both the parenting and financial realities in their families, the Global Generation may be more pragmatic by understanding what is or is not possible to achieve and in what time frame. This will be especially true, if the school system modifies the pedagogy of self-esteem building to one that prepares students to demonstrate the behaviours and the characteristics that the business world expects.

Research abilities

- With research capabilities at their fingertips, The Globes will be expert users of interactive, digital media to source in-formation. However, they may struggle with deeper level research and analysis, because they haven't developed those skills through analytical and critical thinking.

Need for constant stimulation

- It is believed that this generation will not necessarily spend more time using media, but will pack more media exposure into that time frame (e.g. listening to iTunes, while watching a movie, updating their Facebook status and texting six friends at the same time). They will truly be media-multitaskers.[5]

Poor face-to-face communication skills

- Already, there is a concern that Gen Ys don't communicate well face-to-face, and this performance gap will become increasingly apparent with The Globes. However, with the introduction of technologies, such as video-Skype, FaceTime and Halo, face-to-face communication is now being simulated.

Hyper-insistence on individualization

- Since every major facet in their lives can be modified, customized and designed to suit their needs, The Globes will expect high levels of personalization and individualization, even more so than Gen Ys.

The Future of Leadership

This book was designed to provide leaders with nine advanced leadership skills to help them lead teams more effectively today and in the future. The competencies of the nine chapters will always remain core to leadership. However, there are sociological, political and economic factors that are applying constant pressure on organizations. Leaders must continue to think forward. "The way problems arise and the methods of solving them are changing, and not enough companies are adapting to this."[6] Leaders maintaining the status quo will not succeed in the future, and organizations that support this type of leadership style will suffer. Our client, Xerox, has recognized that future leaders will need to be innovative. "They need the capacity to invent and re-invent, and not simply accept and follow the status quo, both in how work is done and the expected outcome."

Leaders will have to unlearn the outdated, and will have to be increasingly more flexible to successfully manage in a dynamic workplace and business environment. Additionally, even though left-brain competencies are currently the most highly valued and are seen as the most operationally relevant, it will be the right-brain competencies, such as intuition and reflection that will give the edge to future leaders."[7] Leaders of tomorrow will have to "think like an anthropologist, have the skills of a family therapist (and) cultivate and trust artistic instincts."[8]

There are six competencies that leaders of the future will need to refine or develop:

1. Information management

Leaders will manage information, rather than generate or control it. Given that the future workforce will be accessing and producing content, leaders will have to accept that information cannot be controlled. Increasingly, there will be few elements that will be personally or professionally private. Organizations will have to redefine the concept of privacy, will have to gain buy-in, and will have to train leaders and employees on the new concepts.

2. Ethics and integrity

The behaviour of leaders will play a significant role, as ethics in business becomes increasingly important. This includes the ethics of how organizations operate globally and in the communities in which they work, as well as the ethics of how each leader interacts with his/her team. The Global Generation will likely be influenced by their skeptical and cynical Gen X parents, who are bound to explicitly or implicitly teach their children to hold leaders accountable.

3. Win-win outcomes

Leaders will have to increasingly ensure that everyone is benefitting from the employment relationship – the organization, the leader, and each employee. The notion of viewing every employee as an investor in the organization and building a win-win relationship with each employee will be fundamental to engaging, retaining and managing employees. For the younger generations, the value of work-life balance will be so important that they will often opt out of a job, if the balance is threatened. Our client, Starwood, has already recognized this trait in Gen Ys which is likely to be even stronger in The Globes: "We need to get away from the cookie cutter approach in how we lead, recognizing that each individual is different. That's really where we've changed our focus in our leadership programs, making them more individual based."

4. Engaging a global workforce

By being aware of the values and characteristics of Gen Ys and The Globes in North America and internationally, leaders will be better prepared to recruit, engage and manage a diverse workforce. "By the year 2020, China is expected to become the second largest economy in the world, developing into a vast consumer market with a sizable middle class," yet very little is known about China's Gen Ys (which consists of about 200 million people born between 1980 and 1989).[9] Whether it's China, India or other emerging world powers, leaders will have to increase their cultural competency as well as understanding the intersection between cultural and generational identities.

5. Intellectual curiosity

The leaders who will be the most successful in the future are those who will be constantly open to the learning process — learning new things, unlearning old patterns and learning some more. Also, innovation and creativity will not remain the sole responsibility of leaders. Instead, leaders will have to disseminate that responsibility to all levels, thus generating fresh new ideas from the ground up.

6. Complex processing of information into action

Future leaders will have to see connections and patterns in complex situations. They will have to understand the interrelationship between stakeholders, departments/business units, and translate them into actions. It will no longer be acceptable to work in silos. Leaders will be expected to fully analyze the costs and benefits of a solution within an integrated horizontal matrix, not just a vertical one. "Silos divide and separate. They often make for good parts that do not work well together. Collaboration comes through unity and sharing."[10] Successful leaders will have to predict what reactions are likely to occur tomorrow, as a result of the actions they or their teams take today.

Notes

Why Upgrade Now?

[1] Conners, R. and Smith, T. (2011). *Change the culture, change the game: The breakthrough strategy for energizing your organization and creating accountability for results.* New York: Penguin Group: 118.

Chapter 1

[1] Conners, R. and Smith, T. (2011). *Change the culture, change the game: The breakthrough strategy for energizing your organization and creating accountability for results.* New York: Penguin Group: 2.

[2] Adapted from Camerson, K. And Quinn, R. (2011). *Diagnosing and changing organizational culture: Based on the competing values framework, Third Edition.* California: John Wiley & Sons, Inc.

[3] Lassister, P. (2011) Employee engagement: Why workplace flexibility will matter. *Workforce Management.* Retrieved August 05, 2011 from http://hiring.monster.ca/hr/hr-best-practices/workforce-management/employee-performance-management/employee-engagement-ideas.aspx: para 16.

[4] ibid., para 18

[5] Friedman, D. (2011). *Workplace flexibility: A guide for companies.* Why Work Works: Families and Work Institute.

[6] Santana, J. (July 14, 2003). Creating supportive, engaging work environment helps fight employee burnout. *Tech Republic.* Retrieved August 3, 2011 from http://www.techrepublic.com/article/creating-supportive-engaging-work-environment-helps-fight-employee-burnout/5035231.

[7] Salovey, P. and Mayer, J. (1990). Emotional Intelligence. *Imagination, Cognition and Personality*, Vol. 913, 185-211: 189.

[8] Parker, G. (2003). *Cross-functional teams: Working with allies, enemies, and other strangers.* Jossey-Bass, San Francisco: A Wiley Imprint: 141.

[9] Newstrom, J. (2002). Making work fun: An important role for managers. *SAM Advanced Management Journal.* Winter, 4-21.

[10] Pink, D. (2009). *Drive: The surprising truth about what motivates us.* New York: Penguin Group.

[11] Silverman, C. (Nov. 19, 2007). *By the Numbers: What Gen Y Wants.* The Globe and Mail.

Chapter 2

[1] Schreuder, AMG and Coetzee, M. (2006). *Careers: An Organisational Perspective*, 3rd Edition. South Africa: Juta & Co Ltd.

[2] Rothwell, W., Jackson, R., Knight, S. and Lindholm, J. (2005). *Career planning and succession management: Developing your organization's talent – for today and tomorrow.* USA: Greenwood Press: 7.

[3] Adapted from: Sharma, S. (n.d.) *Managing employee career development in the 21st century.* HR Crossing. Retrieved October 20, 2011 from http://www.hrcrossing.com/article/270073/Managing-Employee-Career-Development-in-the-21st-Century/: paras 12-14.

[4] Schreuder, AMG and Coetzee, M. (2006). *Careers: An Organisational Perspective*, 3rd Edition. South Africa: Juta & Co Ltd.

[5] Coetzee , M. and Roythorne-Jacobs, H. (2008). *Career Counselling and Guidance in the Workplace. A manual for career practitioners.* Cape Town: Juta & Co: 7.

[6] Carter, G., Cook, K., and Dorsey, D. (2009). *Career-paths: Charting courses to success for organizations and their employees*. Oxford: Blackwell Publishing.

[7] Kroth, M. and McKay, C. (2009). *Career development basics.* USA: American Society for Training and Development: 47.

[8] Yarnall, J. (2008). *Strategic career management: Developing your talent.* Oxford: Elsevier Ltd.

Chapter 3

[1] Armstrong, M. (2000). *Performance management: Key strategies and practical guidelines*, 2nd Edition. London: Kogan Page Limited: 1.

[2] Lennon, D. (April 21, 2011) Pretty good at managing employee performance? What about Bob? *Business Fitness.* Retrieved September 2, 2011from http://dawnlennon.wordpress.com/2011/04/21/pretty-good-at-managing-employee-performance-what-about-bob/: para 23.

[3] Greenberg, R. and Lucid, L. (September 2004). *Beyond performance management: Four principles of performance leadership*. Scottsdale: WorldatWork: 43.

[4] Luecke, R., and Hall, B. (2006). *Performance management: Measure and improve the effectiveness of your employees*. USA: Harvard Business School Publishing Corporation.

[5] Latham, G., Almost, J., Mann, S. And Moore, C. (2005). New developments in performance management. *Organizational Dynamics,* vol. 34(1), 77-87: 85.

[6] Bacal, R. (2004). *The manager's guide to performance reviews*. USA: The McGraw-Hill Inc. Company: 105

[7] Stiffler, M. (2006). *Performance: Creating the performance-driven organization*. USA: John Wiley & Sons: 19.

[8] Adapted from: *Managing employee performance: A guide for supervisors.* (2010).NSPS Transition.

Chapter 4

[1] Gostick, A. and Elton, C. (2002). *Managing with carrots: Using recognition to attract and retain the best people.* New York: O.C. Tanner Company

[2] Wingfield, B. and Berry, J. (2001). *Retaining your employees: using respect, recognition, and rewards for positive results.* USA: Crisp Learning.

[3] Pink, D. (2009). *Drive: The surprising truth about what motivates us.* New York: Penguin Group.

Chapter 5

[1] Cartwright, R. (2002). *Leading 08.10 Empowerment.* Oxford: Capstone Publishing.

[2] Mears, M. (2009). *Leadership elements: A guide to building trust.* USA: iUniverse: 77.

[3] Lee, M. and Koh, J. (2001). Is empowerment really a new concept? *International Journal of Human Resource Management*, Vol. 12(4), 684-695: 687.

[4] Randolph, W. and Kemery, E. (2011). Managerial use of power bases in a model of managerial empowerment practices and employee psychological empowerment. *Journal of Leadership & Organizational Studies*, Vol.18 (1), 95-106.

[5] Maddux, R. (1998). *Delegating for results, revised edition.* California: Crisp Publications, Inc.: 47.

[6] Adapted from: Chan, J. (2004). *Delegating for business success.* USA: AMACOM.

[7] Blanchard, K., Carlos, J. And Randolph, A. (1999). *The 3 keys to empowerment: Release the power within people for astonishing results*. USA: Berret-Koehler Publishers: 48.

[8] Straub, J. (1998) *The agile manager's guide to delegating work*. Vermont: Velocity Business Publishing.

Chapter 6

[1] De Rosa, D., and Lepsinger, R. (2010). *Virtual team success: A practical guide for working and leading from a distance.* San Francisco: Jossey-Bass: 1.

[2] Clemons, D. and Kroth, M. (2011). *Managing the mobile workforce: Leading, building, and sustaining virtual teams.* New York: The McGraw-Hill Companies, Inc.: 3.

[3] ibid: 63.

Chapter 7

[1] CareerBuilder (February 17, 2010). [Survey]. *Working for a younger boss? You are in good company.* Harris Interactive: USA.

[2] Cappelli, P and Novellie, B (2010). *Managing the Older worker: How to prepare for the new organizational order*. Boston: Harvard Business School Publishing.

[3] Ferris, G., Yates, V., Gilmore, D. and Rowland, K. (1985). The influence of subordinate age on performance ratings and causal attributions," *Personnel Psychology* 38, no. 3: 545–557.

[4] Rowe, K (2010). *Managing across Generations*. USA: American Society for training and Development.

[5] Petroulas, E., Brown, D. and Sundin, H. (2010). Generational characteristics and their impact on preference for management control systems. *Australian Accounting Review, No. 54, Vol. 20(3),* 221-240.

Chapter 8

[1] Anderson, D., and Ackerman Anderson, L. (2001). *Beyond change management: Strategies for today's transformational leaders.* California: Jossey-Bass/Pfeiffer.

[2] Ash, P. (2009). Fast and effective change management. *Knowledge solutions, 70,* 1-6. Retrieved September 29, 2011 from http://www.adb.org/Documents/Information/Knowledge-Solutions/fast-effective-change-management.pdf: 2.

[3] Adapted from: Bridges, W. (2010). *Managing transitions: Making the most of change, 3rd Edition.* Philadelphia: William Bridges and Associates Inc.

[4] Beer, M. and Nohria, N. (2000) Cracking the code of change. *Harvard Business Review,* May-June, 133–141.

[5] Axelrod, R., Axelrod, E., Jacobs, R., and Beedon, J. (2006). Bear the odds and succeed in organizational change. *Consulting to Management,* Vol. 17(2), 6-9: 1.

[6] Luecke, R. (2003). *Managing change and transition.* Massachusetts: Harvard Business Press.

[7] Lewis, E., Romanaggi, D., and Chapple, A. (2009). Successfully managing change during uncertain times. *Strategic HR review,* Vol. 9(2), 12-18: 13.

[8] Kotter, J. (1995). Why transformation efforts fail. *Harvard Business Review,* March-April, 59-67.

Chapter 9

[1] American Society for Training & Development. (2010). [Research Study] *Social media: The Millennial perspective*. ASTD: Virginia: 5.

[2] Career Builder. *Will tweet for talent: A user's guide to talent recruitment through social media*. Retrieved August 9, 2011 from http://www.careerbuildercommunications.com/pdf/socialmedia.pdf: 2.

[3] Arbitron/Edison Inc. (2010). *The Infinite Dial 2010: Digital platforms and the future of radio*. [Study]. Arbitron/Edison Research Study.

[4] Career Builder. *Will tweet for talent: A user's guide to talent recruitment through social media*. Retrieved August 9, 2011 from http://www.careerbuildercommunications.com/pdf/socialmedia.pdf.

[5] n-gen People Performance Inc. (2009). [Research Study] *Social Media: Generational Index Report*. Toronto: 2.

[6] Intranet Insider. (March 3, 2009). Building employee engagement with internal social networks. *Communitelligence*. Retrieved August 9, 2011 from http://www.communitelligence.com/blps/article.cfm?page=693.

[7] Jue, A., Marr, J., and Kassatakis, M. (2010). *Social media at work: how networking tools propel organizational performance*. San Francisco: Jossey-Bass: 2.

[8] Azua, M. (2009).*The Social Factor: Innovate, Ignite, and Win through Mass Collaboration and Social Networking*. Boston: IBM Press.

[9] ibid.

[10] Kelleher, D. (2009). 5 problems with social networking in the workplace. *Information management*. Retrieved July 24, 2011from http://www.information-management.com/specialreports/2009_165/social_networking_media-10016208-1.html.

[11] Wilhelm, A. (May 12, 2011). Looking to the future, Microsoft pushes social media in the office. *The next web.com.* Retrieved July 20, 2011 from http://thenextweb.com/microsoft/2011/05/02/looking-to-the-future-microsoft-pushes-social-media-in-office/.

[12] Lake, C. (August 16, 2011). Social media costs businesses $65k a year. Or does it? *Econsultancy.* Retrieved July 27, 2011 from http://econsultancy.com/us/blog/7892-social-media-costs-businesses-65k-a-year-or-does-it?utm_campaign=Skimlinks&utm_medium=affiliate&utm_source=cj: para 8.

[13] Career Builder. *Will tweet for talent: A user's guide to talent recruitment through social media.* Retrieved August 9, 2011 from http://www.careerbuildercommunications.com/pdf/socialmedia.pdf.

[14] Hibbard, C. (February 2, 2010). How IBM uses social media to spur employee innovation. *Social Media Examiner.* Retrieved July 19, 2011 from http://www.socialmediaexaminer.com/how-ibm-uses-social-media-to-spur-employee-innovation/.

[15] Career Builder. *Will tweet for talent: A user's guide to talent recruitment through social media.* Retrieved August 9, 2011 from http://www.careerbuildercommunications.com/pdf/socialmedia.pdf: 5.

[16] Weinstein, M. (February 16, 2011). Gen Y social networking technology surprise. *Training Magazine.* Retrieved July 20, 2011 from http://www.trainingmag.com/article/gen-y-social-networking-technology-surprise.

[17] American Society for Training & Development. (2010). [Research Study] *Social media: The Millennial perspective.* ASTD: Virginia.

[18] Weinstein, M. (February 16, 2011). Gen Y social networking technology surprise. *Training Magazine.* Retrieved July 20, 2011 from http://www.trainingmag.com/article/gen-y-social-networking-technology-surprise.

[19] Whittaker, Z. (November 9, 2010). Forrester study on Generation Y: Social media myths debunked? *ZD NET*. Retrieved July 20, 2011 from http://www.zdnet.com/blog/igeneration/forrester-study-on-generation-y-social-media-myths-debunked/6701.

[20] The Globe and Mail. *Firing on all cylinders with social media.* Retrieved October 20, 2011 from http://www.theglobeandmail.com/report-on-business/careers/firing-on-all-cylinders-with-social-media.

[21] Weinstein, M. (February 16, 2011). Gen Y social networking technology surprise. *Training Magazine*. Retrieved July 20, 2011 from http://www.trainingmag.com/article/gen-y-social-networking-technology-surprise.

[22] Schmeiser, L. (July 7, 2008). The six commandments of social networking at work. *Info World*. Retrieved July 19, 2011 from http://www.infoworld.com/d/adventures-in-it/six-commandments-social-networking-work-845.

[23] American Society for Training & Development. (2010). [Research Study] *Social media: The Millennial perspective*. ASTD: Virginia.

[24] ibid.

[25] Adapted from: Baer, J. And Naslund, A. (2011). *The NOW revolution: 7 shifts to make your business faster, smarter and more social*. New Jersey: John Wiley & Sons, Inc.

What's Next: The Future of Leadership

[1] Brier, J. (October 2, 2010). *Tech-savy 'igeneration' kids multi-task, connect*. USA Today.

[2] ibid.

[3] Wallis, C. (March. 27, 2006). *Gen M: The multitasking Generation*. Time Magazine.

[4] Lyon, E. (Feb.23, 2010). Examining generation Z: Stats, demographics, segments, predictions. Retrieved Nov. 10 2011 from http://sparxoo.com/2010/02/23/examining-generation-z-stats-demographics-segments-predictions/.

[5] Wallis, C. (March.27, 2006). *Gen M: The multitasking Generation*. Time Magazine.

[6] Jamrog, J. (2005). *Leading into the future: A global study of leadership 2005-2015*. New York: American Management Association/Human Resources Institute.

[7] ibid.

[8] Schein, E. (2006). Chapter 23: Leadership competencies – a provocative new look. In F. Hesselbein and M. Goldsmith (Eds.), *The leader of the future 2: Visions, strategies and practices for the new era*. San Francisco: Jossey-Bass.

[9] Stanat, M. (2005). *China's generation Y: understanding the future leaders of the world's next superpower*. USA: Homa and Seka Books.

[10] Losey, M., Meisinger, S., and Ulrich, D. (eds.). (2005). *The future of human resource management: 64 thought leaders explore the critical HR issues of today and tomorrow*. USA: John Wiley and Sons.

References

American Society for Training & Development. (2010). [Research Study] Social media: The Millennial perspective. ASTD: Virginia.

Anderson, D., and Ackerman Anderson, L. (2001). Beyond change management: Strategies for today's transformational leaders. California: Jossey-Bass/Pfeiffer.

Arbitron/Edison Inc. (2010). The Infinite Dial 2010: Digital platforms and the future of radio. [Study]. Arbitron/Edison Research Study.

Armstrong, M. (2000). Performance management: Key strategies and practical guidelines, 2nd Edition. London: Kogan Page Limited.

Ash, P. (2009). Fast and effective change management. Knowledge solutions, 70, 1-6. Retrieved September 29, 2011 from http://www.adb.org/Documents/Information/Knowledge-Solutions/fast-effective-change-management.pdf

Axelrod, R., Axelrod, E., Jacobs, R., and Beedon, J. (2006). Bear the odds and succeed in organizational change. Consulting to Management, Vol. 17(2), 6-9.

Azua, M. (2009).The Social Factor: Innovate, Ignite, and Win through Mass Collaboration and Social Networking. Boston: IBM Press.

Bacal, R. (2004). The manager's guide to performance reviews. USA: The McGraw-Hill Inc. Company: 105

Baer, J. And Naslund, A. (2011). The NOW revolution: 7 shifts to make your business faster, smarter and more social. New Jersey: John Wiley & Sons, Inc.

Beer, M. and Nohria, N. (2000) Cracking the code of change. Harvard Business Review, May-June, 133–141.

Blanchard, K., Carlos, J. And Randolph, A. (1999). The 3 keys to empowerment: Release the power within people for astonishing results. USA: Berret-Koehler Publishers.

Bridges, W. (2010). Managing transitions: Making the most of change, 3rd Edition. Philadelphia: William Bridges and Associates Inc.

Brier, J. (October 2, 2010). Tech-savy 'igeneration' kids multi-task, connect. USA Today.

Camerson, K. And Quinn, R. (2011). Diagnosing and changing organizational culture: Based on the competing values framework, Third Edition. California: John Wiley & Sons, Inc.

Cappelli, P and Novellie, B (2010). Managing the Older worker: How to prepare for the new organizational order. Boston: Harvard Business School Publishing.

CareerBuilder (February 17, 2010). [Survey]. Working for a younger boss? You are in good company. Harris Interactive: USA.

Career Builder. Will tweet for talent: A user's guide to talent recruitment through social media. Retrieved August 9, 2011 from http://www.careerbuildercommunications.com/pdf/socialmedia.pdf

Carter, G., Cook, K., and Dorsey, D. (2009). Career-paths: Charting courses to success for organizations and their employees. Oxford: Blackwell Publishing.

Cartwright, R. (2002). Leading 08.10 Empowerment. Oxford: Capstone Publishing.

References

Chan, J. (2004). Delegating for business success. USA: AMACOM.

Clemons, D. and Kroth, M. (2011). Managing the mobile workforce: Leading, building, and sustaining virtual teams. New York: The McGraw-Hill Companies, Inc.

Coetzee , M. and Roythorne-Jacobs, H. (2008). Career Counselling and Guidance in the Workplace. A manual for career practitioners. Cape Town: Juta & Co.

Conners, R. and Smith, T. (2011). Change the culture, change the game: The breakthrough strategy for energizing your organization and creating accountability for results. New York: Penguin Group.

De Rosa, D., and Lepsinger, R. (2010). Virtual team success: A practical guide for working and leading from a distance. San Francisco: Jossey-Bass.

Ferris, G., Yates, V., Gilmore, D. and Rowland, K. (1985). The influence of subordinate age on performance ratings and causal attributions," Personnel Psychology 38, no. 3: 545–557.

Friedman, D. (2011). Workplace flexibility: A guide for companies. Why Work Works: Families and Work Institute.

Gostick, A. and Elton, C. (2002). Managing with carrots: Using recognition to attract and retain the best people. New York: O.C. Tanner Company

Greenberg, R. and Lucid, L. (September 2004). Beyond performance management: Four principles of performance leadership. Scottsdale: WorldatWork.

Hibbard, C. (February 2, 2010). How IBM uses social media to spur employee innovation. Social Media Examiner. Retrieved July 19, 2011 from http://www.socialmediaexaminer.com/how-ibm-uses-social-media-to-spur-employee-innovation/.

Intranet Insider. (March 3, 2009). Building employee engagement with internal social networks. Communitelligence. Retrieved August 9, 2011 from http://www.communitelligence.com/blps/article.cfm?page=693.

Jamrog, J. (2005). Leading into the future: A global study of leadership 2005-2015. New York: American Management Association/Human Resources Institute.

Jue, A., Marr, J., and Kassatakis, M. (2010). Social media at work: how networking tools propel organizational performance. San Francisco: Jossey-Bass.

Kelleher, D. (2009). 5 problems with social networking in the workplace. Information management. Retrieved July 24, 2011from http://www.information-management.com/specialreports/2009_165/social_networking_media-10016208-1.html.

Kotter, J. (1995). Why transformation efforts fail. Harvard Business Review, March-April, 59-67.

Kroth, M. and McKay, C. (2009). Career development basics. USA: American Society for Training and Development.

Lake, C. (August 16, 2011). Social media costs businesses $65k a year. Or does it? Econsultancy.

Retrieved July 27, 2011 from http://econsultancy.com/us/blog/7892-social-media-costs-businesses-65k-a-year-or-does-it?utm_campaign=Skimlinks&utm_medium=affiliate&utm_source=cj

Lassister, P. (2011) Employee engagement: Why workplace flexibility will matter. Workforce Management. Retrieved August 05, 2011 from http://hiring.monster.ca/hr/hr-best-practices/workforce-management/employee-performance-management/employee-engagement-ideas.aspx

Latham, G., Almost, J., Mann, S. And Moore, C. (2005). New developments in performance management. Organizational Dynamics, vol. 34(1), 77-87: 85.

Lee, M. and Koh, J. (2001). Is empowerment really a new concept? International Journal of Human Resource Management, Vol. 12(4), 684-695.

Lennon, D. (April 21, 2011) Pretty good at managing employee performance? What about Bob? Business Fitness. Retrieved September 2, 2011 from http://dawnlennon.wordpress.com/2011/04/21/pretty-good-at-managing-employee-performance-what-about-bob/

Lewis, E., Romanaggi, D., and Chapple, A. (2009). Successfully managing change during uncertain times. Strategic HR review, Vol. 9(2), 12-18.

Losey, M., Meisinger, S., and Ulrich, D. (eds.). (2005). The future of human resource management: 64 thought leaders explore the critical HR issues of today and tomorrow. USA: John Wiley and Sons.

Luecke, R. (2003). Managing change and transition. Massachusetts: Harvard Business Press.

Luecke, R., and Hall, B. (2006). Performance management: Measure and improve the effectiveness of your employees. USA: Harvard Business School Publishing Corporation.

Lyon, E. (Feb.23, 2010). Examining generation Z: Stats, demographics, seg-ments, predictions. Retrieved Nov. 10 2011 from http://sparxoo.com/2010/02/23/examining-generation-z-stats-demographics-segments-predictions/.

Maddux, R. (1998). Delegating for results, revised edition. California: Crisp Publications, Inc.

Managing employee performance: A guide for supervisors. (2010). NSPS Transition.

Mears, M. (2009). Leadership elements: A guide to building trust. USA: iUniverse.

Newstrom, J. (2002). Making work fun: An important role for managers. SAM Advanced Management Journal. Winter, 4-21.

Parker, G. (2003). Cross-functional teams: Working with allies, enemies, and other strangers. Jossey-Bass, San Francisco: A Wiley Imprint.

Petroulas, E., Brown, D. and Sundin, H. (2010). Generational characteristics and their impact on preference for management control systems. Australi-an Accounting Review, No. 54, Vol. 20(3), 221-240.

Pink, D. (2009). Drive: The surprising truth about what motivates us. New York: Penguin Group.

Randolph, W. and Kemery, E. (2011). Managerial use of power bases in a model of managerial empowerment practices and employee psychological empowerment. Journal of Leadership & Organizational Studies, Vol.18 (1), 95-106.

Rothwell, W., Jackson, R., Knight, S. and Lindholm, J. (2005). Career planning and succession management: Developing your organization's talent – for today and tomorrow. USA: Greenwood Press.

Rowe, K (2010). Managing across Generations. USA: American Society for training and Development.

Salovey, P. and Mayer, J. (1990). Emotional Intelligence. Imagination, Cognition and Personality, Vol. 913, 185-211.

Santana, J. (July 14, 2003). Creating supportive, engaging work environment helps fight employee burnout. Tech Republic. Retrieved August 3, 2011 from http://www.techrepublic.com/article/creating-supportive-engaging-work-environment-helps-fight-employee-burnout/5035231.

Sharma, S. (n.d.) Managing employee career development in the 21st century. HR Crossing. Retrieved October 20, 2011 from http://www.hrcrossing.com/article/270073/Managing-Employee-Career-Development-in-the-21st-Century/.

Schein, E. (2006). Chapter 23: Leadership competencies – a provocative new look. In F. Hesselbein and M. Goldsmith (Eds.), The leader of the future 2: Visions, strategies and practices for the new era. San Francisco: Jossey-Bass.

Schmeiser, L. (July 7, 2008). The six commandments of social networking at work. Info World. Retrieved July 19, 2011 from http://www.infoworld.com/d/adventures-in-it/six-commandments-social-networking-work-845.

Schreuder, AMG and Coetzee, M. (2006). Careers: An Organisational Perspective, 3rd Edition. South Africa: Juta & Co Ltd.

Silverman, C. (Nov. 19, 2007). By the Numbers: What Gen Y Wants. The Globe and Mail.

Stanat, M. (2005). China's generation Y: understanding the future leaders of the world's next superpower. USA: Homa and Seka Books.

Stiffler, M. (2006). Performance: Creating the performance-driven organization. USA: John Wiley & Sons.

Straub, J. (1998) The agile manager's guide to delegating work. Vermont: Velocity Business Publishing.

Wallis, C. (March. 27, 2006). Gen M: The multitasking Generation. Time Magazine.

Weinstein, M. (February 16, 2011). Gen Y social networking technology surprise. Training Magazine. Retrieved July 20, 2011 from http://www.trainingmag.com/article/gen-y-social-networking-technology-surprise.

Whittaker, Z. (November 9, 2010). Forrester study on Generation Y: Social media myths debunked? ZD NET. Retrieved July 20, 2011 from http://www.zdnet.com/blog/igeneration/forrester-study-on-generation-y-social-media-myths-debunked/6701.

References

Wilhelm, A. (May 12, 2011). Looking to the future, Microsoft pushes social media in the office. The next web.com. Retrieved July 20, 2011 from http://thenextweb.com/microsoft/2011/05/02/looking-to-the-future-microsoft-pushes-social-media-in-office/.

Wingfield, B. and Berry, J. (2001). Retaining your employees: using respect, recognition, and rewards for positive results. USA: Crisp Learning.

Yarnall, J. (2008). Strategic career management: Developing your talent. Oxford: Elsevier Ltd.

N-GEN IS YOUR FULL SERVICE TRAINING PARTNER

We deliver training programs in five practice areas:

Sales & Customer Service

We provide foundational and advanced learning on how to improve the customer experience, taking into account that you serve multigenerational customers through your multigenerational workforce.

Leadership

We provide managers at all levels with the tools, techniques and skills required to engage employees, drive organizational performance and increase team collaboration.

Gen Y

We train Gen Ys on generational expectations, and how they can showcase their skills for maximum positive impact in your workplace.

Team Building

We provide employees with an opportunity to explore how to work effectively with all four generations of colleagues, and learn advanced skills that lead to higher levels of collaboration and team performance.

HR Training

We provide HR professionals with strategic knowledge to build effective people initiatives. We support the learning of specific solutions, guiding participants through design, development and implementation.

For full course descriptions, please visit ngenperformance.com.